HAUNTED
WASHINGTON

HAUNTED WASHINGTON

Uncanny Tales and Spooky Spots
from the Upper Left-Hand Corner of
the United States

Retold by Adam Woog

Guilford, Connecticut

Copyright © 2013 by Morris Book Publishing, LLC

Text design: Sheryl P. Kober
Editor: Meredith Dias
Project editor: Lauren Szalkiewicz
Layout: Lisa Reneson, Two Sisters Design

Library of Congress Cataloging-in-Publication Data

Woog, Adam, 1953-
 Haunted Washington : uncanny tales and spooky spots from the upper left-hand corner of the United States / Retold by Adam Woog.
    p. cm.
 Includes bibliographical references.
 ISBN 978-0-7627-7186-8
 1. Haunted places—Washington (State) I. Title.
 BF1472.U6W6665 2013
 133.109797—dc23

                                                           2012050292

Printed in the United States of America

10 9 8 7 6 5 4 3 2 1

This one's for Harriet Baskas, my longtime comrade in arms. Harriet, thanks for being spooked— by so many commitments and so little time— that I got a chance to write this book.

And for my family. Love and happiness, always, to Karen and Leah.

CONTENTS

Contents

Contents

ACKNOWLEDGMENTS

My thanks to the many people who offered their time and knowledge, in particular: Lisa Barksdale, Ferry County Historical Society; Eirena Birkenfeld, Orcas Island Historical Society and Museum; Patricia Brown, Columbia River Exhibition of History, Science, and Technology; Mary Byrd, Dayton Historical Depot Society; Bruce Cowan and Deb Pedersen, Port Townsend; Susan Daniel, Kitsap County Historical Society and Museum; David George Gordon, Port Townsend; Troy Lugenbill, Lynden Pioneer Museum; JoAnne Matsumura, Black Diamond Historical Society; Steve and Judy Metcalf, Olympia; Gregg Olsen, Olalla; Garry Schalliol, Washington State Historical Society; Margaret Shields, Lewis County Historical Museum; Randy Stilson, Olympia; Milton Wagy, Ellensburg Public Library; Janet Wainwright, Seattle; and Steve Willis, Olympia.

INTRODUCTION

What is it about Washington State that makes this place (or at least parts of it) so very spooky? It's tempting to blame the weather, at least in the western half of the state: That region's rain and overcast skies naturally lend themselves to hunkering down inside shelters for much of the year, and sometimes there's little else to do on long winter nights besides tell entertaining stories. (And what's more entertaining than the supernatural?)

But blaming the rain can be, at best, only a partial explanation. There are plenty of places (even in America) that get more annual rainfall, and in truth Western Washington has far more overcast days than ones with actual rain.

Furthermore, gray skies and cool climates don't explain the abundance of ghostly tales on the other side of the "Cascade Curtain"—the eastern part of the state, across the Cascade Mountains. There, the weather is starkly different: hot in summer, cold in winter, and almost always dry.

On the other hand, the extremes in temperature in Eastern Washington can drive its residents to stay indoors a lot—with the same storytelling results.

Or could the underlying reason for the wealth of ghost stories here be the relative isolation of the region, both before and after the early days of European settlement? Did that relative isolation—the feeling that you're out there all alone and relatively unprotected—lead to speculation during those long and spooky nights about the existence of unearthly phenomena?

And then there's the related fact of the state's extremely varied geography and demographics. You've got the dark, foreboding rain forests and sparsely populated islands of the state's far northwest corner; the blue-collar ports and logging towns that dot the southwest part of the state; the rolling hills, near-deserts, and fertile farm- and ranchlands of Central and Eastern Washington; the rugged and remote mountains, especially the Olympic range on the Olympic Peninsula and the Cascade range that divides the state into western and eastern halves; and the rich heritage of the state's Native American tribes. Not to mention the cultural and ethnic diversity of the state's overall population, both urban and rural. Could the unique characteristics of each of these factors contribute to the number and variety of the state's eerie tales?

Frankly, all these explanations seem like a stretch to me. I think the real underlying reason is much more prosaic, and certainly not unique to the region. It's just that people like a good story, especially one that has the potential to scare them out of their socks.

Furthermore, good stories are much more than just entertainment. They also bind societies and groups of people together in profound ways. This is perhaps especially true in the case of stories about subjects that are beyond the understanding of humankind.

Sandy Strehlou, historic preservation coordinator for the town of Friday Harbor on San Juan Island, knows this well. She notes, "Ghost stories, tall tales, and local lore are part of who we are as a community. If nothing else, they are another of the countless shared experiences that make our place—this place—unique. When they are tied to a building or site, they give us another reason to recall history, to wonder about what came before."

And, deep thoughts aside, they're just good stories.

For whatever reason, Washington State has no short-age of places that nurture legends of ghostly happenings, strange sightings, and stories about inexplicable, possibly otherworldly events. This book, *Haunted Washington,* takes a shot at surveying a small handful of these stories.

Writing *Haunted Washington* was way too much fun, but it was not without its frustrations. Specifically, I found it hard to verify a great many of the stories I heard. I have tried to include only material that had a basis in more than just someone's overactive imagination.

My working conditions for inclusion were: A story needed to be mentioned in at least one book or article from a reputable media source and/or involve a well-established legend.

The key word here is "reputable." I am astonished every time I research a book at how some people accept at face value unsubstantiated or incorrect information. Especially with subjects like haunted places and paranormal events, it's too easy to rely on hearsay. So I've tried to avoid regurgitating all of the countless, repetitive versions of "my friend saw something spooky" tales that float around so freely.

(Having said that, I hope I didn't make any embarrassing mistakes myself.)

I'm aware that many colorful ghost tales are invented or inflated by restaurants, bars, and other businesses. Clearly, it's good for business to generate publicity via an otherworldly tale or two. As such, these stories are hardly unbiased. Still, I've included some tales despite their dubious origins—simply because they're good stories.

I have also avoided any direct mention of the state's many paranormal research groups and individuals, because I wanted to avoid any show of favoritism or bias. I appreciate the efforts of these various explorers and wish them only the best.

—A. W., Seattle

Part One

NATIVE AMERICAN LEGENDS, SEATTLE, THE PUGET SOUND ISLANDS, KING AND SNOHOMISH COUNTIES

Chapter 1
Native American
Legends

The Native Americans of the Pacific Northwest have a long and venerable tradition of ghost stories and spooky legends. Each of the dozens of tribes who called—or still call—the Washington State region home has a rich store of them. Here are a few representative samples.

BLUE JAY AND IOI

The Chinook Nation once comprised thousands of linked tribes in what are now British Columbia, Canada, and Washington State, primarily along the banks of the mighty Columbia River. They were a non-nomadic fishing people, dependent on the river's bountiful supplies of salmon, smelt, and sturgeon. They traded extensively with other tribes—everything from furs to dried fish, seashells, and slaves. The Chinook traded with white explorers and settlers as well after contact. The nation's influence in trading was so prominent that the pidgin language called Chinook Jargon was the *lingua franca* for trade in the region.

This story from the Chinook people is about Blue Jay, the mischievous bird trickster who figures in many other Chinook legends, and his sister, Ioi. One day the ghosts went in search of a wife, and one of them fell in love with Ioi. They brought animal teeth as gifts, and the night after the wedding feast they disappeared, taking Ioi with them.

No one saw Ioi for a full year, so Blue Jay decided to visit the land of ghosts to find her. He traveled from village to village and among the animals, asking everyone to show him the way, but no one could tell him until he met one person who promised to take him there.

When he found Ioi in the land of ghosts, she was standing amid piles of bones. She told him that they were her in-laws. Sometimes, she said, the bones would leap up and become human, but they always became just piles of bones if they heard a loud noise.

Blue Jay was able to cause great mischief when he realized that a shout would turn his ghostly relatives into piles of bones. One time, he mixed the ghosts' bones up, putting the skull of a child on an adult torso and laughing at its strangeness when it came to life.

Ioi asked Blue Jay to take her young brother-in-law fishing. The canoes of the ghost people were terrible, full of holes and covered in moss. The things they caught looked to Blue Jay like tree branches, but in the ghost world they were fine salmon. On another fishing expedition, great excitement arose when the ghost people thought that they had found a beached whale. To Blue Jay's eyes it looked like only a large log. The ghost people began stripping the bark off the log, calling it the richest whale blubber they had ever eaten. He shouted and turned the ghosts into piles of bones, then took the blubber for himself, but it still looked like tree bark to him.

Finally the ghost people tired of Blue Jay's pranks, and they convinced Ioi to send him home. She gave him five pots of water and told him he had to return to the land of the living to put out three prairie fires. But Blue Jay ignored her instructions, claiming mischievously that it was good to ignore her because she always lied to him. He did pour the water on the fires, but he didn't take care to see how much was needed to complete the job. By the time Blue Jay reached the last fire, there was no water left and the fire consumed him.

But the dead don't always know that they are dead right away, so when he arrived back in the land of ghosts, Blue Jay did not believe that he was dead. But he acted like a ghost, and he saw things very strangely. Ioi sent her canoe to greet him, and he thought it was the finest he'd ever seen—not a miserable one like he had seen when he was living. Then the ghost people brought him salmon, which before had seemed like tree bark. Now he thought he had never seen such excellent salmon.

No matter what Ioi said, he still didn't believe he was dead because he was convinced that his sister always lied to him. Remembering the pranks he used to play on the ghost people, Blue Jay shouted. But this time the ghosts did not become piles of bones—in fact, nothing happened. Still, Blue Jay wasn't convinced that he was dead. He went to see the medicine man of the ghost people, but he bothered Blue Jay so much that he went insane. The next time Ioi saw him, he was dancing on his head. She said, "My brother is now very dead, and he has lost his mind as well."

In another tale about Blue Jay and Ioi, she told him that he needed to stop playing tricks and find a wife instead. This wife, she said, should be from the land of the dead, the ghost people. Ioi recommended that Blue Jay choose the recently deceased wife of a chief. But she was old, and he wanted a beautiful young woman. So he found the corpse of a beautiful young girl and took it to Ioi. She advised him to take the body to the land of the dead, where it could be revived.

Blue Jay then took the form of a human, which he could do whenever he wanted to. When Blue Jay arrived at the first village of the ghost people, they asked him, "How long has she been dead?" He told them that it had only been a day. But the dead people in this first village said they could not help him. He needed to go to the village where people who were dead for exactly one day could be revived.

Blue Jay continued on his journey, and the next day he arrived at the next village. The same thing happened; the people there asked him how long his bride-to-be had been dead. When he told them it had been two days, they said there was nothing they could do. They could only revive people who had been dead for exactly one day.

So Blue Jay went on and reached the third and fourth villages on the next two days, but he got the same answers. Finally, in the fifth village, he found that the people could help him. They brought his wife back to life. He stayed there for some time, and the ghost people liked him so much that they made him their chief. But Blue Jay got tired of living in the land of the ghosts, so he traveled home with his new bride.

When Blue Jay arrived home, his wife's brother saw that she was alive again. He ran to tell their father, an old chief. The old chief demanded that Blue Jay cut off all of his hair and present it to him as a gift. But Blue Jay refused to do this. The old chief, angered, led a group of his relatives to find him. Just as they nearly caught him, Blue Jay assumed the form of a bird again and flew off to the land of the dead. At that moment, his wife's body fell to the ground. She was dead. This meant that she could travel to meet her husband in the land of ghosts, where he remained in exile.

THE SPIRITS OF BLUE LAKE

The Sanpoil of Central Washington have a legend about a lake near Dry Falls and Grand Coulee that is now known as Blue Lake. One day a man decided to swim to the island in the middle of the lake. Although he was a good swimmer, midway through his journey he suddenly sank.

No trace of him was found for about two weeks, but then his skeleton was found on the shore opposite where he had begun swimming. There was no flesh on his corpse—only bones. The time had been too short for the flesh to have naturally rotted off. Instead, the spirits of the lake had drawn him down and eaten him. No one has gone there since.

SHE WHO WATCHES FROM THE ROCK

The petroglyphs—rock drawings and carvings—at what is now Columbia Hills State Park are among the most interesting and mysterious sights in the state. The park is on the Washington side of the Columbia River near Celilo Falls and the modern town of Wishram, in the region that was once the home of the Wishram tribe. They were relocated there when construction of the Dalles Dam flooded their original location in the 1950s and created Horse Thief Lake. (Thousands more petroglyphs remain underwater.)

The petroglyphs are believed to date back to 1000 to 1500 AD. The most famous of them represents a face, known as Tsagaglalal, "She Who Watches." (Please note: To protect this famous petroglyph from vandalism, visitors can access it only twice a week during certain months, and always as part of an escorted tour.)

There are multiple versions of who Tsagaglalal was and why her striking image appeared on a rock so long ago.

According to one of these stories, one day Coyote, who is often seen in legend as a trickster or shape-shifter, climbed up to a house on a formation now called Horsethief Butte. He spoke with an old woman who lived there. She was the chief of the people who lived below her. He asked her if she had a good life. Was she evil, or did she treat her people well? She replied that she was good and was teaching the people below to build good houses.

She told Coyote that she wanted to be their leader forever. But Coyote told her that the world was changing, and that someday women would no longer be chiefs. Then he changed her into a rock and commanded her to watch over her people and the river forever. She watches over everything in the region to this day, and some say that her huge eyes follow visitors wherever they go.

THE BLACKBERRY SPIRITS

The Klickitats, whose territory once covered what is now Clark County in the southwest part of the state, also have their own ghost stories. One concerns a place of spirits and demons near the modern town of Yacolt. In fact, "Yacolt" is a variation on the Klickitats' name for it: Yalicolb, or "haunted place." This isolated valley site was an important meeting point where trade with other tribes was conducted. Its abundant strawberry and blueberry crops, meanwhile, were highly prized by the tribe, so much so that the Klickitats were not deterred from gathering them even given the presence of demons.

According to one version of the Yacolt legend, a group of children disappeared along a path through the woods, taken by a demon while they picked berries. But a more widespread version of the story concerns an occasion when the tribe fought with another group over fruit-picking rights. According to a book of Indian legends compiled by an early white settler, J. P. Banzer, the Klickitats believed that they had killed all their enemies, but one little girl escaped. Banzer wrote:

> The Klickitat Indians claimed the field and made their annual pilgrimage here to gather berries. On one occasion they found a number of Wilamie Indians, as they called them. A fight started and all the Wilamies were massacred, as they thought, but an Indian girl escaped.
>
> The next year, when the Klickitats returned, they heard someone singing the Wilamie death song and saw a maiden disappear in the distance. Several times they heard her sing. They said she was a spirit, the ghost of her people.

In 1995, Brett Oppegaard of the *Columbian* newspaper commented on a slightly different version of the legend. He wrote, "When the victors returned later for more berries, an eerie song emanated from the trees. The girl was singing a sorrowful serenade to her lost family and friends, and it scared the Klickitats silly. They scattered, sure that the ghosts of the dead berry pickers had risen. It kept the Klickitats away for several moons."

Chapter 2
Seattle

Back in the day, if you told someone you came from Seattle, chances are you'd get a knowing nod and a murmured "Ah, yes, Boeing." Or maybe "Ah, yes, the Space Needle." Nowadays, you're more likely to get a murmured "Ah, yes, Amazon, Starbucks, and Microsoft." Or maybe "Ah, yes, the Space Needle," since that atomic-age structure is still one of the city's best-known icons. And a fair number of people might say, "Ah, yes, that city with all the spine-tingling ghostly legends." Because Seattle has them in abundance.

PRINCESS ANGELINE

Princess Angeline, the doyenne of Seattle ghosts, is the head spirit-in-residence at the Pike Place Market, Seattle's top tourist destination—and one that is frequented by locals too, who appreciate the fresh fruit, vegetables, seafood, flowers, crafts, and other items available there—and who relish the bustling, lively atmosphere of the place. When your author was just a sprat, the market area was pretty spooky in and of itself—the whole waterfront area of Seattle was dilapidated, scary, and potentially dangerous. It has since been cleaned up, and today the market is just great . . . even without the presence of ghosts.

Without a doubt, the market-based legend of Princess Angeline is the most widely told ghost story in Seattle—or all of Washington State, for that matter. The princess is said to haunt the city's famous Pike Place Market—but, by all accounts, hers is a benign presence, not a scary one. It's said that she can sometimes be seen there, stooped and wrinkled, walking with a cane, a handkerchief over her head and a shawl over her shoulders.

When she was alive, Angeline was as close to real royalty in Seattle as that famously casual city is ever likely to get. She was the oldest daughter of Chief Sealth, the leader of the Duwamish tribe of Native Americans. (Sealth lent his name, in somewhat different form, to the city of Seattle.)

The princess was also friendly with many of the white people who settled in the area during Seattle's rough-and-tumble early days. One of them, Catherine Broshears Maynard, gave Angeline her Westernized name; in her native language, Lushootseed, the princess was called Kick-is-om-lo.

Angeline was born in about 1820 in what is now the Rainier Beach neighborhood. At that point, there were virtually no European settlers in the region, and the city of Seattle was not founded until 1851. But by the mid-1860s, a number of white settlers were firmly in place, and they were established enough that they could pass a law forbidding Native Americans from living within the city limits. However, there were exceptions, especially for royalty, and Angeline was allowed to stay. (Her father died in 1866.) For the rest of her days, Angeline lived in a waterfront shack on Western Avenue between Pike and Pine Streets, just below what is now the Pike Place Market, Seattle's venerable (1907) farmers' market. To survive, she dug clams, took in laundry, and sold hand-woven baskets.

Needless to say, the racist policies of those days would hardly stand today. In a 2001 *Seattle Times* article, Leonard Garfield of Seattle's Museum of History and Industry commented, "On the one hand, we revered Native American culture . . . and their efforts to help non-Natives come here, settle and help build a community. At the same time, it was a society where Native people were faced with discrimination and so much had been taken away from them. Our society has never fully resolved those conflicts."

Princess Angeline died in her home in 1896. Today, South Angeline Street honors the memory of Princess Angeline.

At her request, she was buried near her old friend, pioneer settler Henry Yesler (1810–1892), in Lake View Cemetery on the north end of Capitol Hill. In the same cemetery, visitors can also see the grave of martial-arts legend Bruce Lee. Next to it is Lee's son, Brandon, who died on the set of *The Crow* in a tragic turn of events—an accident that some people believe was not an accident at all, but a deliberate murder that has never been solved.

In the century-plus since Angeline passed away, her ghostly presence has been seen many times. Not surprisingly, she's often been spotted in the market itself. According to those who have seen her, she walks along with a basket under her arm or sits alone beside a wooden column in one of the market's lower levels. Even if she isn't there, the area around the column is said to be colder than the surrounding part of the market. Some people further claim to have seen the ghostly image's aura, which can change from white to shades of lavender, blue, and pink.

For unknown reasons, she can also be seen in different circumstances—but only if it's raining. (This is Seattle we're talking about here, after all.) People have reported noticing her walking down one of the steeply sloped streets that go from downtown to the market and the waterfront. According to some reports, this vision is very real-looking— she appears to be a normal, living person—but vanishes if anyone comes close. Furthermore, Angeline's spirit is said to have quite a pungent odor, and reportedly a young boy sometimes accompanies her.

And if all of these sightings weren't enough, the princess has also been seen on the ferryboat between Seattle and Bainbridge Island, out in Elliott Bay. According to legend, Angeline, leaning on her cane, calmly walks onto the ferry and settles down for the ride on one of the ferry's benches. But it's also said that she vanishes into thin air when someone, not realizing who she is, asks to take her photo. In any case, she is never seen getting off the ferry! Before it docks on Bainbridge, she's gone. Where does she go? We may never find out, but it's fun to speculate.

ELSEWHERE IN THE PIKE PLACE MARKET

Princess Angeline is not, by a long shot, the Pike Place Market's only ghost. There's also Frank Goodwin, the market's first director. Apparently, the spirit of old Frank sometimes appears near a restaurant/tavern in Post Alley called the Alibi Room, where he introduces himself and asks if visitors need help with directions—just as he was known to do when he was still alive and kicking.

It's also said that the ghost of Arthur Goodwin, Frank's nephew, is in residence around the market. Arthur took over from his uncle Frank as the market's director, working in that capacity from 1925 to 1941. He then retired to Salt Lake City and died in the mid-1950s, but in recent years people have reported seeing him looking out thoughtfully from his old offices on the market's upper level.

There's also a persistent legend about a woman named Madame Nora who, in the market's early years, told fortunes and performed psychic projection from a place she called the Temple of Destiny. After Madame Nora's death, she began haunting a curio shop called Pharaoh's Treasure, making objects move in the night and otherwise being a nuisance. Eventually, the shop's owner gave the crystal ball that Nora habitually used to the owner of the Market Magic Shop, which still exists in one of the lower levels, and the good madame continues to be in residence there, occasionally showing up to make mischief.

And then there's the little boy who is said to haunt a market shop called the Bead Zone. Some years ago the shop was renovated and a mysterious basket of beads was discovered in a wall. Some people think the little boy gathers them at night to play with them. It's also said that at night he visits the puppets on display in a nearby shop. The Bead Zone has further reported that its cash register opens and closes on its own, and that strands of red beads hanging on a wall once came crashing down for no reason. Co-owner Nina Menon told Stuart Eskenazi of the *Seattle Times*, "I was a healthy skeptic, but seeing was believing. There was no way these beads could have just slid off."

Meanwhile, in nearby Post Alley, a ghost is said to visit Kells, an Irish pub and restaurant. Originally, the building that now houses Kells was the site of the Butterworth and Sons mortuary, which had allegedly been built on a Native American burial spot.

Karen McAleese, a member of the family that owns the pub, swears that on All Saints' Day some years ago she saw a ghostly apparition come out of the Kells kitchen. She told reporter Eskenazi, "He was a tall man who looked like he was part black, with a suit jacket on. He had very thin hands. He walked to the end of the bar and just kind of faded." Kells has also been the location of many other sightings, including that of a little girl, about eight years old with blond or red hair, and a man spotted in a second-story window. It's said that he's a former mortuary employee and wears a cap and suspenders.

And there are plenty of other market ghosts. For one, there's the Fat Lady Barber, who is rumored to have sung her customers to sleep with lullabies, then taken money from their pockets. This was the 1950s, before the market buildings received some much-needed repairs, and one day she fell through rotten floorboards. Because the building drops steeply to the waterfront, the fall killed her. Today, it's said that people cleaning the buildings at night hear otherworldly lullabies coming from a mysterious source. Could they be from her?

Other ghostly happenings in the market include:

- A book—always the same one—that fell from a bookstore shelf every night after closing, even after it was put back in place every day. (The title of the book has apparently been lost in the mists of time.)
- Ghosts who can be heard fighting in the walk-in freezer of Mr. D's Greek deli.
- The inexplicable appearance of an overwhelming fragrance of perfume in the Market Theatre (a venue for many eclectic events). The same location has been the source of the laughter of ghostly children.
- A stable boy named Jacob, a victim of the 1918–19 worldwide influenza epidemic who lived in a now defunct toy store and was known to throw things at people. The poltergeist stopped when the owner made a little bedroom for him, which apparently calmed him down.
- The ghost of "Mae West," a raunchy, elderly woman who was a market fixture until her death in the 1990s,

usually dressed in purple and wearing a crocheted hat with beer labels. (Personal aside: Your author remembers her well.) According to legend, Mae West's ghost can still be seen and heard wandering around the area. Furthermore, it's said that her ashes were scattered around a fruit tree in a market courtyard—and that, ever since then, the tree has begun to bear fruit, something it had not done for years. Today, it's said, people swear they sometimes see a purple glow around the tree.

THE GEORGETOWN CASTLE

Beyond the Pike Place Market, there's Georgetown—one of the oldest neighborhoods in Seattle. Its early background, from when it was a wide-open part of town near the port, has long given it a raffish (if slightly seedy) charm, and recently it's become a haven for artists seeking cheap rent. But it's also the site of some colorful hauntings, with chills whose sources predate even the arrival of European settlers.

For one thing, Georgetown is built over some ancient Native American burial grounds, and Chief Seattle, whose Duwamish tribe once lived in the region, reportedly spoke of his people's "shadowy returning spirits"—a clear indication that these ghosts might still be around. Then, in Seattle's rough-and-tumble early days in the late nineteenth and early twentieth centuries, the neighborhood served as both an industrial center and a red light district. As many as twenty-four saloons operated all day and night just in Georgetown, and there were plenty of rooming houses for workers from nearby factories—not to mention a variety of houses where ladies of the night were on duty, ready to meet the romantic needs of loggers, gamblers, miners, fishermen, and sailors who passed through.

Today the neighborhood's most famous building is the Georgetown Castle, an ornate three-story house built in the early twentieth century by a wealthy gambler named Peter Gessner. (Gessner also owned the Central Tavern, which is still a landmark in Seattle's Pioneer Square.) The Castle was—and still is—a lavish display of fancy architecture, with gables, bays, dormers, a wraparound porch, and a round turret. Inside, it's replete with nine high-ceilinged bedrooms and a theater.

The many ghostly stories told about it are confusing and conflicting, but here are some details: Gessner allegedly built the place for his young bride, Lizzie—but she took up with another man, so he converted the house into a gambling den and brothel. In part, this was because Gessner was being sued for letting minors gamble in Seattle, where authorities periodically cracked down on this ordinance and on vice in general. Instead of shutting down, Gessner simply moved his operations to Georgetown, which was then outside the city limits.

Gessner died in 1903, just one year after building the Castle. The cause: drinking carbolic acid. Newspaper reports at the time suggested that he committed suicide over his failed marriage, but his friends suspected foul play. In any event, the coroner decided not to hold an inquest. Lizzie Gessner and her paramour married and, amid scandal, moved into the mansion that had been built in her honor.

The house next changed hands when Dr. Willis H. Corson, formerly the superintendent of what was then the King County Hospital and Poor Farm, bought the place as a retirement home. After Corson's death the house went through several more incarnations: gentlemen's club, speakeasy, brothel, and boardinghouse. In time the ornate house fell into serious disrepair—and that was when its neighbors, and its residents, began to notice some strange things happening around the now-derelict building.

Two of these people were Ray McWade and Petter Pettersen, who lived in the mansion in the 1970s. One day, the two men discovered a small, walled-off room that seemed to them to be unnaturally cold. They could also hear ghostly noises of brawls upstairs—where, it goes without saying, no one could be found. Then, according to one report, a hungry houseguest once walked into the kitchen of the Georgetown Castle and wondered aloud where the bread was—at which point a loaf of the stuff rolled out of the cupboard and onto the kitchen counter. One morning, Pettersen found a dead cat on the steps. He buried it, but the next morning the body of the unfortunate feline was back on the porch.

Furthermore, McWade and Pettersen reported seeing a ghost they dubbed the "Spanish Lady." Dressed in black and looking "totally insane" (as Pettersen told the *Seattle Times* in 1983), she grasped at her throat with one hand and struck out at people with the other. Later, from memory, Pettersen, who was an accomplished artist, painted the Spanish Lady's likeness. One day, an elderly acquaintance stopped by and remarked that the portrait looked just like her great-aunt Sarah, who had met a bad end in the Georgetown mansion.

The ghost of another Sarah, who was Gessner's daughter-in-law, and/or a prostitute named Mary Christian, also haunted the place. (There are different stories about exactly who this unfortunate woman was.) At any rate, according to legend, Sarah/Mary had an illegitimate child. She doted on the baby, but the infant's father did not. He killed it, buried it under the front steps, and locked the distraught woman in the mansion's turret, where she went mad and died a horrible death.

Since the days when McWade and Petter Pettersen lived there, the mansion has changed hands several times. While working on a major restoration project for the Castle, its current residents have reported a number of otherworldly occurrences. These include sudden chills, unexplained banging on doors, doors that won't stay shut, and heavy, ghostly footfalls. One houseguest complained that an unseen force pushed him down the stairs at one o'clock in the morning.

Many explanations have been put forward for this and other spooky events at the Georgetown Castle. Could it be the ghost of a pauper, one of many cremated on the grounds of the old hospital? The victims of airplane crashes from nearby Boeing Field? Or maybe Peter Gessner himself?

Today, the Castle has been restored to its original beauty, and a splendid garden surrounds it. In 2008, one of its current residents told *Seattle Met* magazine, "I think the spirits are appeased. I think they're pleased with all the work we've done."

Still, there's always a possibility that any lingering ghosts around the Castle are not very happy with all of the changes that have been made over the years. Who's to say?

THE CHINATOWN-INTERNATIONAL DISTRICT

Seattle's population has always had a notably strong Asian contingent, and today one of the city's liveliest neighborhoods is the Chinatown-International District. (When your author was a kid, it was known simply as Chinatown, despite the presence of many different ethnic groups, notably a vibrant Japanese community. Today, in these more politically correct times, it's informally known just as the "I.D.")

Many of the Asian cultures that are part of today's I.D. have, since ancient times, had well-established and deeply felt traditions and legends about ghosts and other supernatural beings. So it's no surprise that Seattle's I.D. is a good representative of the many Chinatowns around the state that continue to flourish—and that harbor haunted spots.

According to legend, for instance, something from beyond our everyday world was resident for many years in Ruby Chow's restaurant at the corner of Broadway and Jefferson. This Seattle institution was named for its owner, who was also the first Asian member of the King County Council. She continued to be a major force in regional Asian-American politics until her death in 2008.

As for that ghost: Persistent legend has it that Chow's restaurant was haunted. According to one report, an assistant to the cook (Ruby's husband, Ping) saw a ghost in the basement, came flying up the stairs, and quit that day. On another occasion, an unseen force allegedly jostled one of Ruby's cousins while she was carrying a tray of dirty dishes. And the story goes that a teapot suddenly tipped over on its side—by itself—and the tea that spilled onto the floor formed a perfect question mark. Ruby herself, meanwhile, sometimes claimed that a supernatural black shadow once pinned her to the floor on her stomach.

Outside of Seattle history, Ruby Chow is perhaps best known as an early patron of someone who went on to international fame: the legendary martial artist and actor Bruce Lee. Born in San Francisco and raised in Hong Kong, Lee returned to the States in 1959, still a teenager, and settled in Seattle. He was a rowdy young man, and his parents arranged for him to live in a room above their friend Ruby's restaurant and work there while attending Edison Technical

School (now part of the Seattle Central Community College campus). The story goes that Lee, a budding martial arts expert, once fought with the same spooky black shadow that had earlier attacked Ruby Chow.

In time, as his millions of fans know, Bruce Lee would be a household name by his early thirties. Lee is buried in perhaps Seattle's most illustrious eternal resting place: Lake View Cemetery on Capitol Hill. Next to his grave is that of his son, Brandon Lee. (This is the same cemetery that houses the body of Princess Angeline. See page 11.) The Lees' resting places are among the most-visited graves in the Seattle area (the champion being the grave of Jimi Hendrix in Renton's Greenwood Memorial Park).

There have been reports of Bruce Lee's ghost sitting on a small bench or cross-legged on the ground in front of his grave. It's also said that he never speaks or moves; he just sits there quietly. Furthermore, there are reports that the spirit of Brandon Lee appears sometimes in various locales around the International District, dressed in black—but that he disappears when approached.

In addition to Ruby Chow's (which is now closed), another International District institution is the East Kong Yick Building, built in 1910 by a consortium of local Chinese businessmen. Since 2008 the building has housed the neighborhood's main museum, the Wing Luke Museum (formally called the Wing Luke Museum of the Asian Pacific American Experience). Today, the East Kong Yick Building is a handsomely restored brick structure, but in the years before its transformation its condition had become sadly dilapidated. It was perhaps this shabby appearance that led to the numerous ghostly stories about it, mostly revolving around the building's Asian residents. In a 2005 article in the *Seattle*

Times, reporter Paula Bock commented, "Empty, eerie, the upper floors of the East Kong Yick Building house pigeons, peeling plaster and the spirits of Asian immigrants who worked the canneries, logging camps, fields and orchards before the world wars."

In Bock's article, the museum's then-executive director, Ron Chew, commented that he was planning a traditional ceremony to honor these spirits. When asked if there were ghosts in the building, Chew replied:

> You can sense a presence. Most other construction projects have a ground-breaking ceremony, but we're having a blessing ceremony . . . to acknowledge the spirits of the men who walked these corridors and lived difficult lives. You sort of embrace the past and use their stories, certain lessons, to direct you to the future. It's part of the strong ancestor worship that's in Asian cultures. . . .
>
> [These residents experienced] loneliness, prostitution, gambling, all the elements of what a bachelor society is. They relied on each other for companionship, translation services, job referrals. They didn't migrate into the rest of society as much as we do now. There were severe class and racial boundaries.

When asked about his personal beliefs in spirits, Chew commented:

> I'm no ghost-seeker type, but when I first moved in, I'd go to sleep, wake up in the middle of the night, sense a presence, turn on the light and not see anybody. Later on, I realized it was the spirit

of my grandfather. . . . My uncle, who was killed in World War II [is buried nearby]. My father worked in the old Hong Kong restaurant here for 30 years. My mom worked in Seattle Glove, a sewing factory on 12th Avenue. She wanted to be around to see the opening of the museum, but you know, her body gave out. Anyway, I'm comforted that I have four spirits watching over me, watching over this project.

Elsewhere in the I.D. is Maynard Alley South, just off South King Street. It's a small alleyway, and not very appealing: dark and dank, and poorly lit even when the sun is shining brightly. In short, it's the perfect breeding ground for stories about otherworldly apparitions. And stories there are.

The presence of ghosts is most strongly felt near a pair of doors with a terrible history. Today, the doors are shut with a rusty padlock and covered in graffiti—just another example of urban neglect, and easily overlooked unless you're specifically hunting up ghosts. But they hide quite a story. *Seattle Post-Intelligencer* writer Kery Murakami comments that these doors "would look foreboding enough even without their history. They are in a desolate alley in the International District, where feathers fall from the pigeons in the broken windows of the abandoned apartments above the doors, and where a woman in a parka rummaged through a commercial garbage bin, and a man in his pajamas stood smoking a cigarette."

The history that Murakami is talking about stems from the days when those forlorn doors led to the Wah Mee Club. The Wah Mee was an illegal gambling den—and the site of the worst multiple homicide case in Washington State history.

During the Prohibition Era in the 1920s, the Wah Mee was an elegant speakeasy that catered to a high-rolling clientele, mostly made up of some of the Chinese community's wealthiest and most prominent citizens. As of the 1980s, it was still in operation as a gambling den, and it still catered to many of the wealthiest members of Seattle's Chinese community. But then came the Wah Mee Massacre.

Late in the night on February 18, 1983, amid Chinese New Year celebrations, Kwan Fai "Willie" Mak and his accomplices, Wai-Chiu "Tony" Ng and Benjamin Ng, staged a robbery. Mak, the ringleader, came up with the plan because he had incurred thousands of dollars in debt. He and his accomplices knew everyone in the den, so they didn't bother to wear masks; they knew they would have to kill everyone. They tied up the fourteen people there, shot them, and made off with tens of thousands of dollars. Thirteen of the fourteen victims died on the spot, but one man, Wai Y. Chin, survived and was able to identify the killers. All three were sentenced to lengthy prison terms.

So are the ghosts of the dead gamblers still haunting the place? Maybe. It certainly is true in the minds of some people. Djin Kwie Liem, who owns Liem's Pet Shop next door to the former gambling den, told Murakami, "It's not scary being next door to the Wah Mee. But some people refuse to work here because of it."

Even if you like animals and would love to work in a small pet store, would *you* want to work next to the site of such a horrendous massacre?

THE SMOKIN' GHOST OF BALLARD

Although it's changed radically in recent decades, Ballard was once a blue-collar neighborhood known for its Scandinavian immigrants and its close connections to the fishing and logging industries—two crucial areas of commerce during Seattle's earliest years. Back in the early twentieth century, Ballard was a powerhouse in this regard; among its other distinctions, it was the world's largest producer of cedar shakes.

Even today, now that it's multicultural and even hip, Ballard retains elements of a strong Scandinavian tradition. Check out, for instance, the Nordic Heritage Center, the annual Viking Days celebration, the strong whiff of lutefisk you can sometimes discern along Market Street, and the many residents whose names end in "-son" or "-sson."

Some Scandinavian spooks may also travel here and there among those living residents—or so it's said. One location with a prominent reputation for haunted happenings is Smokin' Pete's BBQ restaurant, on the corner of 20th Avenue NW and 65th Street NW.

A sign hangs over the bathroom door at Smokin' Pete's: WARNING—BEWARE OF THE GHOST. The sticker was there before the current restaurant opened. It apparently dates from the time when the building was a butcher shop called, appropriately, the Butcher Shoppe. Reported sightings from those days include the presence of a mysterious short man with a black hat, standing with his horse (!) in what is now the restaurant's dining room. According to another story, strange things started happening following the death of the father of one of the butcher shop's owners. Notably, the bathroom door kept getting locked—from the inside.

Smokin' Pete's co-owner, Julie Reinhardt, points out that the uncanny events continue to this day. Writing on her blog, She-Smoke.blogspot.com, Reinhardt comments:

The other night I was working late on a Monday. We recently decided to be closed on Mondays during the fall and winter, to give ourselves and the business a break. I find I love to work in the peace and quiet.

Only the other night, it wasn't at all quiet.

I've never liked working at night alone at Smokin' Pete's. It's in part because of the stories, and in part because old buildings make noises, but also because of something else. Something not super scary or menacing, but definitely something more.

I heard that something the other night. I was in the bathroom when something, or someone BANGED the door. Hard. It jolted me out of my end-of-the-day brain drain, and immediately all senses went to high alert. This wasn't a door creaking from a sudden gust of wind. The bang I heard was so hard and definite that the door shook, echoing for a few moments after.

"Hello? Who's there?" I called, quickly gathering up my things.

Silence.

I was outta there faster than you could say, "I AM NOT AFRAID."

Don't worry. I've never heard or seen hide nor hair of any ghosts during business hours. But whoever is there likes the place to themselves once the open sign is turned off and the dishes are done.

I understand. Maybe we, me and the ghost that is, can find a way to share the lovely silence on Mondays.

Blues harmonica player and world-renowned edible bug expert David George Gordon has his own ghost story from a gig at Smokin' Pete's. He told your author:

When we first played at Smokin' Pete's, during our last set, I hit a super-high note on the harp and this beer can jumped into the air and then fell to the floor—and there was nobody at the table! My guitarist and I both saw this happen, and we were astounded. The staff told me about the ghost and how they had to call a locksmith several times to open one of their two unisex bathrooms that had been inexplicably locked on the inside. Turns out, that was the bathroom where the former owner (who passed away) used to go to read the newspaper during quiet times on the job.

THE BURNLEY GHOST

Capitol Hill has long had a somewhat Bohemian, slightly unconventional charm, and today's version maintains that reputation. From the inlaid dance steps on the Broadway sidewalk and the stately homes atop it (dating from Seattle's early days) to its hip restaurants and reputation as a safe haven for the gay community (it's where the city's Gay Pride Festival originated), there's always something happening on Capitol Hill.

And, of course, that includes ghostly legends.

One of the best known and most enduring of these tales concerns an apparition at the Burnley School of Professional Art. Founded in 1946 by Edwin and Elise Burnley, the Burnley School was situated for many years on Capitol Hill at

9th and Pine on Capitol Hill. (In 1982 the building became part of Seattle Central Community College and the Burnley School became the Art Institute of Seattle, which is currently located downtown on Elliott Avenue.)

Beginning in the 1960s, reports began to emerge about strange events at the Burnley School. Doors opened by themselves. Unseen presences dialed phones. Staff and students arriving in the morning found the furniture rearranged, when the school had been supposedly empty and locked the night before. Even coffee percolated by itself (and this, as the late Seattle historian Walt Crowley pointed out, was "before Mr. Coffee!").

Ghostly footsteps also echoed down empty halls. According to *Seattle Times* reporter Paul Andrews, people have reported that the ghost begins his approach "by walking slowly up the old wooden stairs, thock, thock, thock, like the ticking of a clock. He'll proceed down one of the narrow, high-ceilinged corridors, his feet making sandpapery sliding sounds on the worn plank floors—a sound that can make skin crawl and swallowing difficult. Then he'll turn into a room and maybe take a seat at a desk, maybe rearrange pens and papers or shift in his chair."

The most popular theory to explain these spooky events concerned the legend of a high school student who, years earlier, had died after falling down the school's steep rear stairway. However, there's no shortage of other stories, including that of a teenager who was killed in 1913 in a fight after a basketball game. (Hoops was just starting to become widely popular at that point in the sport's history.)

In any case, someone nicknamed the ghost "Burnley." During the 1960s, Crowley noted on Historylink.com, a medium reportedly tried several times to contact the spirit. One séance was interrupted by a loud crash in an upstairs bathroom. A window had been broken by a huge rock, far too heavy to have been thrown from the alley below. A session of automatic writing (a form of writing that is said to come from the subconscious, and so is believed to aid in contacting the other world) led the medium to the building's basement, where a hole was found that the rock fit into perfectly. Otherwise, digging around the hole revealed nothing but the skeleton of a small animal. Crowley noted, "Later missives from beyond made special but cryptic references to the spirit's left shoelace. This writer attended a follow-up séance on a truly dark and stormy night in 1968. Nothing terribly supernatural occurred, but it turned out that the left shoelace of every male attendee had broken that day. I've worn loafers ever since."

ELSEWHERE ON CAPITOL HILL

Near the Burnley School, another spot with a reputation for ghostly presences is the Capitol Hill United Methodist Church building, on 16th Avenue East near E. John Street, which is now a historic landmark. The ghosts of Reverend Daniel Bagley and his wife, Susannah, are said to visit on occasion. Bagley, an important figure in the early history of Seattle, was the church's minister, and his wife headed its women's auxiliary.

Daniel Bagley died in 1905, his wife in 1913. Today, Seattle honors the clergyman with, among other things, Bagley Street, the University of Washington's Bagley Hall, and Daniel Bagley Elementary School. Perhaps their spirits can be discerned in these places, but it's in the Methodist church (now) that they're most often reported.

These spirits are said to be translucent, blue-lit, hologram-like visions. According to one story, Susannah

Bagley appeared in a flowing gown and asked a startled man how to get out. Thunderstruck, he pointed to a door, but she left through a third-story window.

A deacon and sexton for the church told *Seattle Times* reporter Julie Schuster, "I opened the door—I was doing my nightly rounds—and there he was. He was looking past me. He didn't seem to see me. I've never seen anything like it. He was translucent, sort of like those holograms."

Also on Capitol is the Harvard Exit movie theater, a handsome brick building dating from 1925. Once owned by the culturally oriented Women's Century Club (which still meets there), today the Exit is well known as Seattle's most elegant movie house. The theater's main lobby recalls its glory days in the 1920s, complete with a grand piano, a fireplace, and period furniture.

But the Exit is also the location of various spooky legends. It's said that at least three or four female spirits and a couple of male spirits are in residence. One of the males, said to be portly, distinguished-looking, and translucent, has been nicknamed Peter. One witness claimed that she spotted Peter near the screen, enjoying himself tremendously. It's said that another male spirit has a British accent. One woman, so goes the story, is the spirit of none other than Bertha K. Landis, Seattle's only female mayor (to date) and a prominent member of the Women's Century Club. One of these ghostly women allegedly has blurry features and wears an old-fashioned dress. The reasons given to explain the hauntings vary considerably, including the murder of a man in the building that stood on the property before the present structure was built. Another version concerns a woman who, for unknown reasons, suffocated in the building during the 1940s.

One of the many reported incidents concerns a former theater manager who heard strange noises upstairs one evening while he was in the main lobby. A door slammed shut, followed by a loud scream and the sound of running. He ran to investigate and, halfway up the staircase, ran into an employee who was hurtling down. She was visibly shaken and agitated, but she was able to tell the manager that she had just seen a headless woman in a flowing dress suspended in the air about six feet off the ground.

Another tale from the Harvard Exit involves another former manager. Early one evening, she was preparing to open the theater as usual. When she opened the doors to the elegant downstairs lounge, a fire had been lit in the fireplace. Nothing strange about that—except that no one else was in the building, and employees were forbidden to leave a lit fire unattended. This fire had obviously been burning for a while. Sitting in one of the lobby's high-backed chairs, meanwhile, was a woman. She wore a long, old-fashioned, flower-print dress made out of a thin material. Her hair was short and tightly curled, an old-fashioned style. She was reading a book and, according to the manager, the woman lifted her head and looked straight at her for a moment before fading into nothing.

The manager immediately called the owners of the building and the janitor, who all said there had been no fire in the fireplace when they left earlier in the day. The manager later commented to this author, "I will tell you that experience changed my life in many ways. It confirmed for me that at the very least there is something beyond our known world."

Other reported incidents at the Harvard Exit involve film canisters that have been misplaced or reorganized. Movie projectors have started running on their own. On one occasion, an employee arrived to find the movie already playing—with the projection room locked.

And a former projectionist, while on the job one evening, allegedly noticed that a stool between the booth's two projectors was vibrating. The vibrations grew more agitated until the stool stood on one leg and spun around for a moment before settling down again to its normal inanimate state.

GREEN LAKE

Green Lake Park, west of the University of Washington, was created as part of a greenbelt system designed for the then-young city by the famous landscape architect Frederick Law Olmsted. (Olmsted also created New York City's Central Park and many others around the country.) Green Lake Park is adjacent to Woodland Park and the zoo, and (not surprisingly) it surrounds Green Lake. The lake annually draws thousands of walkers, runners, rollerbladers, and bicyclists to the three-mile path around it, and with them the attendant pleasures of exercise, conversation with friends, and nature- and people-watching. It's one of the most-used public spaces in Washington State.

But Green Lake does not have an unblemished history. It was also the scene of a notorious murder. Thereby hangs a gruesome tale—based on an historical incident and complete, of course, with a ghost in residence.

On June 16, 1926, a pair of workmen noticed a pair of slippers. Investigating further, they found a bloody trail, a white felt hat, and the body of a young, nearly naked woman. Subsequent police investigation turned up evidence of a struggle in the water and a jagged, blood-smeared rock on the shore.

The victim was Sylvia Gaines, age twenty-two, who had recently moved to Seattle to live with her father and step-mother near Green Lake. Her case became one of the most sensational in Seattle's history. When Sylvia's stepfather, Wallace "Bob" Gaines, was arrested for the murder, it was revealed that he and Sylvia had been having what the prosecutor at Gaines's trial called a "strange and unnatural" relationship, and that they had recently argued. Bob Gaines maintained his innocence, telling reporters, "I loved my daughter more than anything on earth. I was affectionate toward her. Why shouldn't I be?" But at the trial the prosecutor stated, "Fear of exposure—fear that he would lose the object of his lust—that's what prompted the murder of this girl."

The jury returned a death sentence in just over three hours. Gaines proclaimed his innocence until the day he was hanged. But the ghostly presence of Sylvia Gaines, so they say, lingers on.

That bodiless ghost—just a head, according to some reports—can be seen in the evening hiding behind bushes and trees, lingering around a memorial to Sylvia Gaines. The memorial is a grove of poplar trees planted on what is now Gaines Point, a jut of land on the lake's eastern shore. This grove, near what is today the Green Lake Community Center, is a sad reminder of one of Seattle's most notorious murder cases.

SEATTLE HOTELS

As a popular tourist destination, Seattle has a wide variety of hotels, from the elegant and expensive to the not so elegant and expensive. Hotels are time-honored locations for ghost stories; so, not surprisingly, a number of ghostly legends are attached to many of them.

One concerns the elegant Sorrento Hotel on First Hill (aka Pill Hill, so called for its concentration of hospitals and other medical facilities). According to legend, a ghostly presence known as the Red Lady haunts the third and fourth floors of the Sorrento. There have also been reports of inexplicable footsteps elsewhere in the building, and at the establishment's luxurious restaurant, the Hunt Club, guests have reportedly seen glasses moving by themselves.

Meanwhile, just north of downtown is a neighborhood called Belltown. Formerly a scruffy haven for artists and various illegal or semi-legitimate activities, Belltown in recent decades has become a very hip location, full of chi-chi restaurants and expensive condos (as well as continued semi-legitimate activity, alas).

One of Belltown's ghostly attractions is the sophisticated Hotel Andra, formerly the Claremont, at the intersection of Fourth Avenue and Virginia Street. The ninth floor of the Andra is allegedly home to occasional and inexplicable party noises, reminiscent of the Prohibition era. (The building was built in 1926 at the height of Prohibition.) The ghostly sounds from times past include hot jazz, breaking glassware, and loud, jolly voices—but the sounds disappear when anyone tries to investigate. There have also been reports from the Andra of other eerie happenings, including a levitating paperweight that, according to witnesses, suddenly came down with a crash on a glass-top desk. There's also a tale that a worker took a fatal fall from the hotel sometime in the 1960s, and that his spirit still haunts the place.

Farther south on the corner of Third Avenue and Cherry Street is the Arctic Building, built in 1916 and once home to the prestigious Arctic Club. Many of the swank Arctic Club's members had made their fortunes during the Alaska-Yukon

Gold Rush and continued to do business there. Today the building is the luxurious Arctic Club Hotel, and it is on the National Register of Historic Places. The edifice is instantly recognizable from the street if you look up; carvings of walruses, complete with tusks, decorate the third floor's exterior walls.

The building may be elegant, but it also has a gruesome history, including a tale about the ghost of a man who fell to his death from a high window—and whose death may have been murder.

The story about this mysterious death—did he jump or was he pushed?—dates from 1936, when the country was in the midst of suffering through the Great Depression. Rubye Louise Zioncheck, the wife of US Representative Marion Zioncheck, was sitting in a car parked outside the building, where the congressman had an office. She was waiting for her husband to join her—but then her wait ended.

Suddenly, a man fell from a window of the Arctic Building. The body hit the pavement only a few feet in front of Mrs. Zioncheck. She jumped out of the car, ran over to the body—and started to scream.

She had good reason to scream. The dead man was her husband.

The next day a newspaper reporter wrote, in rather purple prose:

[W]hen Congressman Marion A. Zioncheck killed himself before her eyes last night, something snapped inside this young bride, the former Rubye Louise Nix. And in an instant, she was transformed from a brave, carefree, laughing girl into a grief-stricken woman, both as old and as ageless as death itself. All dressed in white for the postal employees banquet she had expected to attend with her husband, she presented the tragic picture of a bride at a funeral as restoratives were administered to her at King County Hospital.

Police found a rambling, sometimes incoherent note in Zioncheck's office in Room 517. It addressed his despair over the woes of the economic depression: "My only hope in life was to improve the condition of an unfair economic system that held no promise to those that all the wealth of even a decent chance to survive, let alone live."

Zioncheck's death was ruled a suicide. Supporters of this theory pointed to his increasingly erratic behavior in the months before his death. But some of Zioncheck's family members insisted that he'd been pushed. He'd been cheerful before the incident, they said, not despondent. On the other hand, Zioncheck's brother-in-law, who was in the congressman's office at the time and who apparently held quite different political views, said he saw Zioncheck dive out the window: "If I'd been just a second quicker I could have caught him, I only missed him by a foot when I grabbed for him as he jumped."

Today, Seattle Police Captain Neil Low says he finds this story hard to believe. Low told PI.com reporter Chris Grygiel in 2011 that the brother-in-law provided too many details to make a convincing story. Low maintains that no one who witnessed such a terrifying event would have remembered so much. The policeman commented that if he had worked the case the witness "would have some explaining to do. . . . I [think] this stinks to high heaven."

The officer's interest in the case was piqued when he was assigned to the city's Domestic Violence/Sexual Assault unit and worked out of Zioncheck's old office. Low occasionally heard the elevator coming up to his floor—but nobody had called for it and nobody was in it. The policeman asked around, thinking the elevator was broken, and was told by building employees that it often comes to the fifth floor all by itself . . . because the ghost of the congressman is apparently still trying to reach his office.

Chapter 3

The Puget Sound Islands

Closer to Seattle than the San Juans, the islands in Puget Sound have, over the years, changed from rural enclaves of fishermen and farmers into suburbs of Seattle, accessible by the region's public ferry system. Commuting between Seattle and an island home is an excellent way to decompress from the intensity of city life. It's also an excellent place to get some shivers from the stories told about its resident spirits.

WHIDBEY ISLAND

Whidbey Island is the largest of this grouping of islands—in fact, it's one of the largest islands in the contiguous United States. Whidbey (pronounced "wood-bee") has another distinction: It plays host to several grisly ghost stories. And none is grislier than the saga of Isaac Ebey, his decapitation, and his missing scalp.

Ebey's history on the island dates from 1850, when he staked out 640 acres of land in the central part of the island. Homesteading there was a tough way to live, not least because Native American tribes from the north regularly visited, generally hoping to pillage other tribes. White settlers like Ebey were also tempting targets for raids by these northern tribes.

The white intruders fought back, not surprisingly. A major turning point in this ongoing conflict came late in 1856, when a US Navy gunboat, the USS *Massachusetts,* opened fire on a group of Indians camped out on the island. There is some doubt as to which tribe they were from, but it was probably either Haida or Kake, and they may have come from as far away as what is now southeast Alaska. In any case, twenty-eight Native Americans died in the attack by the *Massachusetts.*

The following year, the tribe returned to exact its revenge. They first targeted one of Whidbey's most prominent citizens, Dr. John Kellogg, but he was off the island when they arrived. So the raiders attacked the Ebey home instead, knowing that its owner was also a prominent man in the white community—and he was no friend to Native Americans.

The raiding party fatally shot Isaac as he stood in his doorway. Then they cut his head off and took it as a prize when they headed home. At some point they removed his scalp, including his ears and hair, and discarded the rest.

A friend of the Ebey family, Captain Charles Dodd of the Hudson's Bay Company, heard of the incident and vowed to retrieve the scalp. After several unsuccessful attempts, Dodd was able (as noted by the WaGenWeb genealogical organization) to trade "six blankets, 3 pipes, 1 cotton handkerchief, 6 heads of tobacco, 1 fthm. [6 feet] cotton" for the scalp.

After bringing the gruesome item back to Port Townsend, a town on the mainland, Dodd presented it to Isaac's brother, Winfield. Winfield later wrote in his diary (as reprinted on a website maintained by the Sunnyside Cemetery on the island), "[N]ow his poor head . . . returns to his home. The skin of the head is entire contained, the ears and most of the hair. The hair looks quite natural. It is a sad memento of the past."

Isaac's much-traveled scalp remained in the Ebey family's possession, although for unknown reasons it was never buried with the rest of his body in the family plot on Whidbey. It continued to move around, and its last verified location was California's Bay Area. Its present whereabouts are unknown.

Not surprisingly, the creepy story of Isaac Ebey's scalp has given rise to an equally creepy ghost story. Today, people say, they can sometimes see a translucent blue light moving around the upstairs windows of the dilapidated, long-deserted Ebey family cabin. An extension of this legend has it that Ebey's ghost occasionally emerges from the cabin to wander around the yard, cradling his long-decapitated head in his arms.

More recent strange and ghostly incidents have been reported on the island. One eerie legend comes from Naval Air Station Whidbey Island near Oak Harbor, which is widely reported to have a haunted building.

That would be the Base Exchange (PX), housed in a facility that was built, in 1942, as a hangar for some of Whidbey Island's wartime fleet of seaplanes. The building has since been broken up into several amenities, including a snack bar, a food store, and a large retail store available to military personnel and their families.

Legend has it that in the late 1940s, after the end of World War II, there was a terrible accident: A mechanic was killed when he got caught in the propeller of a plane on the ground. In the years since that gruesome tragedy, a number of people say they have observed a man dressed in mechanics' overalls, walking on the catwalks toward the back of the PX building's storage space. This in itself would be very strange indeed; allegedly, it would be impossible for a person to get onto those catwalks without being noticed. In any case, no one has ever been able to get close to the ghostly man—he disappears when they try.

Not just that—it's reported that employees opening the stores in the morning sometimes find piles of clothing scattered around. On occasion, these clothes are carefully arranged as if they had been worn by someone who just disappeared while lying down—right up to the socks inside the shoes. Again, a mystery: If it was a hoax, how could someone have broken into the facility after hours without disturbing the sturdy locks that protect it?

Then there's the Captain Whidbey Inn, which dates from 1909 (although its charmingly mismatched rooms and halls have been remodeled and added to over the years). The inn is located in the town of Coupeville, overlooking Penn Cove (home of the famous mussels of the same name). For years, there have been persistent reports of unexplained events at the inn, including mysterious body impressions on beds, disembodied girlish laughter, and more.

Furthermore, it's said that some specific areas of the inn—especially Rooms Six and Eight—are hot spots for ghosts, because they are regularly visited by the spirit of a quiet, unobtrusive elderly lady. Some people have suggested that she's the wife of the island's namesake, Joseph Whidbey, a British naval engineer who was part of George Vancouver's expedition in the 1790s to explore the Pacific Northwest coastline. However, this identification would be at odds with the reported sightings, since it's typically claimed that the spirit is dressed in a Gay '90s–style dress—thus putting her about one hundred years ahead of ladies' fashion. Is she a fashion-forward otherworldly entity, or is she the spirit of someone other than Whidbey's wife?

BAINBRIDGE ISLAND

And then there's the military ghost of Fort Ward on Bainbridge Island. Until late 1941, there was nothing particularly noteworthy about Fort Ward—it was just a typical US Navy base. But on December 7, 1941, the base became a small but crucial part of history—an incident that has since led to persistent rumors of an otherworldly presence.

December 7, 1941, of course, was the date of the surprise Japanese attack on the US Pacific Fleet's base in Pearl Harbor, Hawaii—"a date," in President Franklin D. Roosevelt's famous words, "which will live in infamy." The attack resulted directly in America's entry into World War II, an event that would in time dramatically alter global history.

Fort Ward played its role in that history thanks to one of its facilities, a top-secret radio office known as Station S. Since 1940, when the threat of imminent war with Japan began to loom large, Station S had been regularly eavesdropping on coded Japanese radio transmissions. However, neither it nor any other American radio facility knew that a large Japanese naval force had secretly moved into position off Hawaii.

Then, on December 6 (Hawaii time), Station S intercepted a shocking teletypewriter message, sent from Tokyo to the Japanese ambassador in Washington, DC. This message, known as the Fourteen-Point Memo, stopped short of formally declaring war. However, it ordered the Japanese ambassador to break off his ongoing diplomatic negotiations with US Secretary of State Cordell Hull.

When Station S intercepted the message, the news was transmitted to Navy headquarters in Washington, DC. At the time, however, passing along such transmissions was time-consuming. It required decoding the message, translating it, and encrypting it again—not to mention sending it via sometimes balky radio transmission lines. It was thus some time before a cryptologist in DC realized that the message might signal an imminent attack.

Meanwhile, Tokyo's original transmission of the message was also delayed in reaching its ambassador in DC. By the time he and Hull met (on December 7, Washington time) Japan's forces had already attacked Pearl Harbor. The next day, America declared war.

In the years since that string of tragic events, the building that once housed Station S has become a private home, one of several such homes, within the boundaries of the state park that occupies the once-active naval base. Since 1989, the former Station S building has been the home of Sarah Lee, an historian and activist on the island. As such, it's a very special place. An anonymous writer for the *Bainbridge Island Review* noted in 2008, "A house is rarely just a house. But Sarah Lee's house comes with something extra." That something extra? A spirit. Lee herself wrote in an article for *Cryptolog*, "There are ghosts in our house. Well, we've never ever actually seen them, but we know that they're here. After all, it's impossible to walk into our house and not sense the 'ghosts' of the hundreds of young men and women who worked here from 1910 through the '50s."

As it happens, Lee is a Morse code enthusiast, and she told the *Bainbridge Island Review* writer that one day she was in the basement when she felt and heard a Morse code message come through the old-fashioned rotary phones she's had converted to transmitters. It was so strong, she stated, that she could hear and feel the reverberations: "And it was this very weird time travel sense of what it might have been like."

A reporter for the Tokyo Broadcasting System television network, Nao Tase, experienced something similar when she interviewed Lee for a documentary about Japan during World War II. Quoted in the *Bainbridge Island Review* article, Tase commented, "[W]e went down to the basement where the incinerator was. And I could sort of imagine people taking all the [confidential] papers and throwing them into the incinerator and burning them."

Tase continued, "And then, I felt like I could feel people typing. I guess I'd seen so many messages and had heard people talking about it . . . It kind of felt like I was hearing the radio and the messages being typed out."

Although Sarah Lee expresses skepticism about the presence of ghosts as they are traditionally portrayed, she does assert that any building with a long history likely contains some trace of the people who once lived and worked there. She told the *Review* reporter, "The thing that makes [my house] so important is that you can take history and say, okay, from 1939 to 1941, these were the people who were here. Or, you can make it come alive. That's what this house still being here allows you to do. Because it's kind of like a magnet, for the people who used to work here, a magnet for Tokyo Broadcasting System, and a magnet for history. And whether that's the ghosts or not, I don't know."

Lee expanded on this idea in an essay (also for the *Bainbridge Island Review*) that was published in 2011. She urged her audience to explore similar historical spirits around the island: "I don't mean chain-rattling ghosts. If ghosts are the stories and the history each person leaves behind, then I have hundreds of them. And you probably do too [if] your house or building is at least 50 years old."

Chain-rattling or not, it does seem clear that Bainbridge Island has its fair share of inexplicable and eerie events.

Chapter 4
King and Snohomish Counties

Seattle is far and away the dominant part of King County; for one thing, its urban density, when combined with its suburbs, makes it the most heavily populated county in the state and the fourteenth most populous in the US. But there's much more to the region than that.

The name of the county has an interesting history: It was originally named after William Rufus King, a prominent politician who briefly served as the thirteenth vice president of the US. In 1968, a motion was introduced to change the county's namesake from its original—who had been a slave-owner—to Dr. Martin Luther King Jr. This proposal eventually became law, although the formal name change did not take effect until 2005. Meanwhile, a public vote changed the county's logo from a crown to an image of Dr. King.

North of King County is Snohomish County. Its topography is varied and always interesting, from the shores of Puget Sound to the green and fertile farmlands around Arlington, and to the rugged Mount Baker National Forest, which sprawls over roughly half of the county. The great industries of Washington's past—logging, farming, and fishing—have in some ways ceded ground to more modern ways of life—a prime example being the enormous Boeing plant near Everett. But at least a tantalizing hint of the past—and with it a host of ghosts from days gone by—always remains.

THE ISLAND THAT SINKS NIGHTLY

Mercer Island (where your author grew up) lies in the middle of Lake Washington. It is named for an early family of white settlers, the Mercers, who used it as a place to fish, hunt, and pick berries. For centuries before the arrival of the Mercers, however, the local Duwamish Indians knew about the island and its supernatural nature.

In fact, the Duwamish refused to set foot on it after dusk. To them, the island—which was often shrouded in a shadowy fog—was a sacred place of spirits, and it was best not to disturb them. Also, according to one legend, the Native Americans believed that the island sank into the lake every night and reappeared in the morning.

Today, according to a 2008 article in the *Mercer Island Reporter,* the island still has some eerie spots. One of them is the only cemetery known to have existed on the island, on Appleton Lane off East Mercer Way.

It was originally the home of a pioneer family, the Olds. When the family's patriarch and matriarch, Charles and Agnes Olds, died in the late 1890s, they were buried at the top of the family's apple orchard. Three more Olds family members eventually joined them. The gravestones and bones have been removed, but some people say that Appleton Lane (which has since been developed into a string of modern homes) still has a creepy vibe.

Then there's the island's southernmost point, which is today known as South Point, logically enough. But South Point was once nicknamed Murder Point. The reference is to a notorious double homicide that occurred there in 1886.

According to some versions of this story, two men, James Colman and George Miller, had a longstanding disagreement over a plot of land on the island. Colman was a land title investigator who confronted Miller over the settler's questionable claim to the land. After the confrontation, the title investigator left by rowboat accompanied by a young boy. (Their exact relationship is unknown.) The two were bound for Seattle to file charges against Miller—but neither of them was seen alive again.

Detectives investigating the disappearance found a boat covered with blood near South Point, and the pair's bodies eventually washed up on shore. They had been murdered. Miller was tried and acquitted three times, but he apparently confessed on his deathbed. The anonymously written *Reporter* article notes, "Whether the murdered souls ever found rest remains a mystery." Meanwhile, the spirits of Colman and his companion are still said to linger at Murder Point.

But there's another version of the South Point story, one that involves the spirits that lived in the area's trees. Megan Carlisle, the archivist of the Eastside Heritage Center, comments, "The point was called 'Stripping,' and an old man had once angered the supernatural creatures who lived in the stumps there by stripping off their clothing (tree bark)."

And then there's the eerie tale of Calkins Landing, in the neighborhood of Mercer Island known as East Seattle.

An ornate Victorian-style structure, the Calkins Hotel, stood there. It was built and operated by C. C. Calkins, a lawyer who owned most of East Seattle. Calkins envisioned an affluent community there with a business district, school, church, and other amenities. In the meantime, his hotel catered to well-off vacationers (including President Benjamin Harrison).

At times, it was also the site of death and disaster. For one thing, there was an incident involving two men who reportedly rowed away from the dock, one of them armed with a revolver. By the time the boat returned, one had been shot dead, supposedly in an accident.

But worse luck was to come for Calkins and his family. According to a Historylink.org article by Alan J. Stein, "the Panic of 1893, a nationwide economic depression, severely hurt his business. Soon after, the Calkinses lost a newborn child. Mrs. Calkins and her daughter then went on vacation to recuperate, but while doing so, the young girl accidentally fell from a hotel window and was killed. . . . Mrs. Calkins died soon after."

The grief-stricken and financially strapped Calkins left the area for good a short time later, and the hotel remained an empty shell until 1902, when it was sold. Over the next few years, it served as school for delinquent boys and as a sanitarium for narcotics addicts.

By 1907, however, the building again became a summer hotel. But this phase of its life was short-lived: In the summer of 1908, an employee angry over a scolding stuffed oily rags into a chimney. Fire broke out, and the hotel burned to the ground.

The Calkins Hotel was never rebuilt. But, according to legend, the spirit of the young Calkins girl who fell to her death still lingers there and can sometimes be felt in the evening around the hotel's old location, as an eerie feeling that something is out there . . . just beyond reach.

And then there's a legend surrounding another vintage Mercer Island building, in this case one that's still around: the Roanoke Tavern, which dates from 1914. Over the years there have been a number of urban legends about haunted happenings in this venerable place. Owner Dorothy Reeck, quoted in the *Reporter* article, says that she has yet to experience anything spooky. But she is open to the possibility: "If there are ghosts, they're a lot of happy ones. Nothing scary."

Elsewhere on the island is Youth Theatre Northwest, which is housed in what used to be North Mercer Junior High. The organization today focuses on theatrical productions by and for children and young adults. But it is also the location of a legendary ghost.

The story goes back to the 1970s, when the facility was still a junior high. A teenager committed suicide by driving his car into a wall there. Today, actors and others working at the theater late at night report feeling a strange and inexplicable presence in the building. Among the alleged manifestations is one that came during a paranormal investigation in the boys' dressing room. When one member of the investigatory team wondered in a loud voice if something bad had happened there, a door inexplicably slammed shut.

THE GHOST OF THE ROLLING LOG AND MORE

Heading east along I-90 from Mercer Island, a spook hunter will want to stop in the town of Issaquah. At 58 East Sunset Way is a building that has had a checkered career—and a persistent ghostly legend.

It started life as the Grand Central Hotel, built in 1903 when Issaquah was a stopover point for rail passengers. This was followed by incarnations as Issaquah's post office, a bordello, a speakeasy, and a five-and-dime store (not necessarily at the same time). After years as a derelict building, it was remodeled early in the present century and incorporates a tavern next door. The Rolling Log, formerly the Grand Central Café, has been an institution among locals since the 1930s—and, the locals say, to three resident ghosts as well.

Owner John (Jack) Lydon, quoted in an article in the *Seattle Weekly,* is a skeptic: "I've been here 35 years, and I've never seen the ghost." One of the Log's bartenders, Julie, concurs, "I have not seen the ghost, but a lot of people have. I know someone died in the bathroom, but that was five years ago. The ghosts were before him. There are three of them."

Meanwhile, a former bartender named Carlos says that he saw plenty of paranormal activity there. Quoted in the *Weekly* article, he said, "I've opened and closed that place way too many times. About 3:15–3:20 is when things start getting iffy." Carlos says he's actually sensed four spirits: "There's a cowboy near table #2—the table on the right-hand side of the door. And an 'all-in-black' guy. And there's a little girl. She's all over the bar; a prankster."

The fourth? A spirit that's not as benign as the others. "I got this bad energy around 4:00 like 'It's time to go,'" Carlos asserts. "He messes with people, dropping boxes, making noises. I thought at first that it was the people that live upstairs, but the noise was coming from the bar."

Elsewhere in Issaquah, also on East Sunset Way, is a 1940s-vintage building that has housed Ankhasha's Temple of the Western Gate, operated by psychic reader and self-described "spiritual advisor" Ankhasha Amenti. The building has had a persistent legend of ghostly activity associated with it. This activity has included unexplained footsteps, specters that can pass through walls, and pranks played by spirits (including moving objects around and turning lights on and off).

The most haunted spots in the building, Amenti states, are the back stairs and attic. In 2011, Amenti told Issaquah reporter Kendall Watson, "Up in the attic, workmen have heard strange noises . . . and thought they had seen some-one when no one was there. [The spirits] seem to enjoy playing tricks on people."

Originally an auto shop, the building was used for a variety of businesses over the years, including for a time a consignment shop. In 2009, Amenti told a reporter from Seattle TV station KCPQ that when she moved in she "could notice there were spirits here in the building. I felt the vibrations of the spirits." Amenti added that her belief is that there are two ghosts, Alex and Dick—the spirits of the auto garage owners.

One of the workers who renovated the building, Steve Randolph, also noticed something eerie. Randolph told KCPQ that he was a skeptic until he saw "a little lady, this tall, with a black coat and hat standing right by that post. Just as I set my tool down she was gone."

BLACK DIAMOND

South of Issaquah, the little town of Black Diamond—now a semi-rural suburb of Seattle and Tacoma—got its name from one of the earliest industries in the region. The Black Diamond Coal Mining Company of California set up shop there in the 1880s, transporting what it obtained from the earth to the docks of Puget Sound and on to San Francisco.

Many of the men who worked Black Diamond's coal seams in the early days were European immigrants, and their tough job conditions all too often led to early deaths. As might be expected, many of these men are buried in the town's cemetery. JoAnne Matsumura of the Black Diamond Historical Society commented to this author, "The percentage of miners buried in this historic cemetery is overwhelming."

All of this, Matsumura adds, has led to unconfirmed reports that the miners buried in the cemetery have been heard talking to each other. A 2011 story by Dennis Box in the *Covington/Maple Valley/Black Diamond Reporter* notes that there have been reports of swinging lights at night (the kind of thing a miner's lamp might make). According to one source, one such light was seen for several minutes among trees and about eight feet above the ground. Box noted, "If you catch sight of a strange light near the Black Diamond Cemetery, it may not be from a streetlight."

Another report recounts whistling in the cemetery heard on foggy or dark nights. And still another account states that a white horse has been spotted in the cemetery. Our advice: Consider staying away from the Black Diamond Cemetery, unless you're really determined to see something strange.

SNOHOMISH COUNTY

Up in Snohomish County, in the town of Snohomish itself, the people at the Oxford Saloon, which dates from 1910, have their own legends about the place's hauntings. According to them, the upstairs rooms at the Oxford were once part of a brothel, and today the spirits of various "soiled doves" from those days still like to visit. Among them are three ghosts in particular, nicknamed Kate (or Katherine), Mary, and Miss Precious. About Katherine, the City of Snohomish website states, "Dressed in early 1900 attire, it is assumed that it was she who recently requested an Oxford Saloon T-shirt from an employee who turned around with the shirt but Kathleen was gone. We guess ghosts don't carry much cash."

Another story you'll hear if you hang around the Oxford is a legend about a policeman named Henry. Killed in a knife fight in the stairwell, Henry is still said to linger in the tavern. The reported encounters with him include a number of mischievous events, including employees hearing their names called in an empty room, objects falling by themselves from the bar, and wall pictures mysteriously found crooked.

Over at the Cabbage Patch Restaurant, the place's owners claim that several spirits have been sensed in the upstairs dining room, on the stairs, and coming in through windows upstairs. As is common with reports of ghosts in restaurants, it's said that employees have witnessed dishes and glasses moving on their own.

According to legend, the main spirit in question at the Cabbage Patch is that of Sybill Sibley, who fell down the stairs and broke her neck in the early 1900s. (Another version of the story is that she died elsewhere in the 1930s and later, rather creepily, followed her family to Snohomish.)

Meanwhile, there's an alleged spirit over at the building that for years housed the venerable Snohomish Public Library. (The library is now in a more recently constructed building.) The legend concerns Catherine McMurchy, the chief librarian from 1923 to 1939. The story goes that her ghost can be seen or heard walking in the basement after hours.

Despite having been a gainfully employed librarian, Catherine was apparently penniless when she died and was buried in Seattle in an unmarked grave. The City of Snohomish's website points out that the library started a fundraising project to buy a proper headstone for Ms. McMurchy's grave, and that the city's librarians hope that she will continue her afterlife at the library's new location.

Not all former or current residents of the town of Snohomish are willing to believe the stories about the ghosts in their home, though. Writing on the Roots Web genealogy site, Carroll Clark states, "Funny though, we 'kids' who knew

Catherine McMurchy from the mid-1920s 'til she retired haven't heard of her ghostly activities until 'newcomers' began writing and telling stories about it. Same thing with the Oxford Tavern which was familiar to us, but it was only detected among the 'latecomers' that 'Madame Kate' & her crew began 'occupying' the place. Is it possible that we 'old timers' that used to be kids don't have the 'awareness' to detect this phenomena?"

Elsewhere in Snohomish County, the historic Everett Theatre in Everett—the oldest operating theater in the state—has its own ghost story. That would be Smilin' Al. In 2011, *Everett Herald* writer Theresa Goffredo noted, "If you are not familiar with Smilin' Al, he's the ghost that has allegedly been haunting the theater since the early 1990s. He's named after the legendary vaudevillian and movie star Al Jolson who once performed on that historic stage."

That appearance by the famous performer was in 1906, just five years after the theater opened. After his shows there, Jolson was left stranded when his manager skipped town with the box office receipts. Nine years later, he returned and bygones were apparently bygones—he cheerfully related to the audience the story of his earlier troubles in the town. This spirit of forgiveness may explain why today's Smilin' Al is a friendly ghost.

Over at the Everett Inn, it's said that a ghostly man is also in residence, walking the hallways while dressed in a janitor's suit. It's not clear who the alleged spirit might be, although it appears he may be a maintenance man who remains in the building even though it has changed hands several times.

And in the town of Maltby, the tiny Maltby Cemetery has been the subject of persistent urban legends about ghosts.

Some people have reported visible spirits there, dressed in antique clothes. Others report being assaulted by unknown forces. But the eeriest of the rumors floating around about the Maltby Cemetery have to do with what's known as the 13 Steps to Hell.

Legend has it that these steps lead to the underground tomb of a wealthy family. The rumor is that anyone who goes down the steps will find a dirt wall and, on turning around, will see a horrible crowd of agonized ghosts. A variation on this tale suggests that the steps actually lead to the site of a cave used for Satanic rituals.

The notorious steps have been bulldozed over because so many people—drunken yahoos, mainly—came to check out the site. But people—again, mainly drunken yahoos—still show up periodically and wander around the cemetery in hopes of finding the eerie spot. In a *Seattle Times* article by Diane Mapes from 2005, one veteran Pacific Northwest ghost hunter commented, "There are all kinds of legends about this little cemetery, but . . . there are no steps. All you'll find is a cemetery surrounded by woods with all these beer bottles all over the place. I guess the more you drink—the more ghosts you see."

Part Two

NORTHWEST WASHINGTON

Chapter 5
Tacoma

Tacoma is the third-largest city in the state (after Seattle and Spo-kane). The name is a variant of Tahoma, the Native American name for what is now called Mount Rainier. Tacoma is due south of Seattle on Puget Sound and its port facilities on busy Commencement Bay rival those of its neighbor to the north. In addition to its port activ-ity, Tacoma was once a thriving lumber town, with its smelly pulp mills giving rise to the "Tacoma Aroma." Fortunately, this epithet is no longer valid; the lumber mills have been shut down for years, and Tacoma smells just fine. These lumber mills were just places of work. On the other hand, Tacoma is the location for many, many spooky stories of eerie events and supernatural spirits.

THE PANTAGES THEATER

In 1918, Greek immigrant Alexander Pantages opened a beautiful theater on Broadway in downtown Tacoma. It was designed by B. Marcus Priteca, a distinguished architect who designed many of the Northwest's finest theaters. Priteca modeled the Tacoma Pantages on the design of an ornate theater in the Palace of Versailles outside Paris.

Now restored to its full glory and renamed the Broadway Center for the Performing Arts, the building today is a bus-tling cultural venue—and the place is said to be haunted as well. (The same thing is said about many of the other remaining Pantages theaters in the United States and Can-ada, for that matter.)

Alexander Pantages, who was originally from Greece, was a shrewd theatrical producer in the late nineteenth and early twentieth centuries. After a checkered early career history (including a stint helping dig the Panama Canal and a failed attempt at riches during the Alaskan Gold Rush), Pantages moved to Seattle and opened his first theater, which presented a wide variety of traveling vaudeville shows and other performances. In time, he expanded the entertainment he provided, turning to silent movies as vaudeville began dying out. He was notably successful: At its peak, the Pantages chain was America's largest independently owned circuit of movie and vaudeville theaters.

This is where the ghost stories start to come in. Pantages's financial backing came from his paramour, Kathleen Rockwell, known to all as Klondike Kate. Kate was a well-known dancer around the Pacific Northwest, who, according to the Broadway Center website, "held miners spellbound with her flame dance and took their breath away when she appeared in a $1,500 French gown. [She said,] 'We were vendors of laughter and music to men who were starved for beauty and gaiety. And we gave good measure for all the gold the miners showered upon us.'"

She had met Pantages in Alaska during the Gold Rush, and they remained together for years—until she accused him of stealing money from her and marrying another woman. The case led to a breach-of-promise suit, which was apparently settled out of court. According to some sources, Kate had already lost all her money bankrolling Pantages at one point, and she died penniless and forgotten.

Jump to modern times and the persistent legend of an otherworldly spirit that apparently hangs around Tacoma's

Broadway Center. By some accounts, this ghostly apparition is a stunning beauty dressed in the height of fashion from the early twentieth century. She has often been spotted walking or sitting alone in the balconies. Is she Klondike Kate? Some say so.

Other spirits have also been spotted in the former vaudeville theater. Some people have said, for instance, that a ghostly presence there has been known to assist those patrons who arrive late to their seats. The ghost helpfully stops the patrons at their proper seats with an unusual signal—a blast of cold air.

And that's not the only apparition people say they've observed around the place. There's a carved face, said to be a likeness of Pantages himself, above the stage—and, it's reported, the carving's features sometimes change. Its expression depends on the quality of the performance.

Furthermore, the theater's head carpenter has been quoted as saying that he has twice seen a ghostly man around the place, watching carefully as the theater closes after a show. Some say it's the spirit of Alexander Pantages himself, coming around to see how the old place is doing.

THE PAGODA

The ornate building in Tacoma known as the Pagoda, on scenic Five Mile Drive, was built in 1914 as a terminus for its trolley system. Modeled on a building from feudal-era Japan (but made of cement, not wood), it is set amid lush gardens that feature pools, a waterfall, a footbridge, cherry trees, azaleas, and rhododendrons. Remodeled in the years since its construction, including an extensive restoration after a 2011 fire, the Pagoda is now used for weddings and other happy events.

So it may be a place of joyous celebration. But there's also a dark legend connected with the Pagoda. As an unnamed reporter for the *Tacoma News Tribune* put it in 2011, "Not only is the pagoda first in the hearts of countless brides and grooms, it also has a place among followers of the occult and ghost-chasers."

The story goes that back in the 1920s a small passenger ferry ran from a dock by the Pagoda. A pair of newlyweds was in the habit of taking the trolley to the Pagoda, where the female half of the couple would get on a little ferry to visit her parents on nearby Vashon Island. The husband would take the trolley home, and then return in the evening to greet his wife. Records are sketchy, but the boat she took was probably part of the private Tacoma Ferry Company's fleet.

One day, according to legend, the husband was standing as usual at the dock, and he could see the ferry approaching—but then it began to take on water. As the vessel began to capsize, he took out a pocket telescope and watched in horror as people went overboard—including his wife, who quickly sank under the weight of her heavy clothing.

Grief-stricken, he ran downstairs to the marble men's restroom and shot himself in the head with a small pistol.

(Of course, this raises several questions. If he was so grief-stricken that he would shoot himself, why didn't he at least try to swim out in a rescue effort, even if he knew the ferry was too far away? And what was he doing carrying both a pocket telescope and a pistol?)

Pesky problems like these aside—let's not wreck a good story with questions—the tale has led to a number of reports of ghostly events. Among them: footsteps, made by what sound like hard-soled shoes, around the building after dark—especially down the stairs on the east side of the building and in the vicinity of the men's room. Loud sighing noises, the sound of drenched clothing hitting the building's floor. Inexplicable cold spots have also been reported.

Author's note: A widely told story connected to Five Mile Drive, where the Pagoda is located, concerns the spirit of a teenage girl who was murdered there in 1986. The unsolved, all-too-real, and relatively recent killing was extensively publicized in news media at the time. Out of respect for the girl's family, the story is not included here.

A TACOMA TIDEFLATS GHOST, A PHARMACY PHANTASM, AND MORE

Back in the days of the Great Depression, shantytowns of homeless people sprang up in a number of cities across the country. They were dubbed Hoovervilles, a sarcastic reference to hapless President Herbert Hoover, whose fiscal policies were widely held to have spurred on the economic crisis. One of these makeshift towns was on the then undeveloped Tacoma tideflats. It's said that the ghostly spirit of a transient who lived there still walks around in the area, dressed in ragged clothes of the period and accompanied by a dog. The man doesn't acknowledge the presence of a human, but the dog begins to bark loudly. Some say that the ghost is that of a man who committed suicide in desperation while engaged in a standoff with the police.

In nearby Steilacoom is another spot well known for its occult apparitions. W. L. Bair opened the venerable Bair Pharmacy on Lafayette Street in 1895, and he was succeeded by his son, Godfrey "Cub" Bair. Their drugstore/hardware store later became a cafe, most recently an establishment called the Bair Bistro.

The story goes that a spirit, presumably Cub, hangs around the place and causes mischief such as items flying off shelves, otherwise normal appliances that suddenly stop working, and light fixtures that inexplicably move around on their own. Apparently, Cub just doesn't like new things cluttering up his place. One of the restaurant's owner/managers told a reporter for the *Tacoma News Tribune*, "He worked here the longest, and is very finicky about changes. He doesn't like all the changes we are making."

Also in Steilacoom, along Commercial Street, was another venerable business: the E. R. Rogers Restaurant. Edwin R. Rogers was a seaman and merchant from Maine who settled in Steilacoom, prospered mightily, and in 1891 built a seventeen-room mansion overlooking Puget Sound.

According to legend, a female ghost haunts the place. Perhaps she is Catherine Rogers, who was either E. R.'s widow or stepdaughter (accounts vary). Or she may be Hattie Bair, Cub Bair's wife, who according to legend killed herself upstairs. In any case, Cub Bair's family and the Rogers family were intertwined. The Bairs apparently bought the place from the Rogerses in 1920 and made it an inn, though this chronology is unclear.

At any rate, after many years as a restaurant the building now houses law offices—and ghosts. Among the reported otherworldly events in the house are lights turning on by themselves after the building is closed up at night, alarm systems that are inexplicably tripped, ghostly faces in the windows, and the sight of a woman's leg—just the leg, mind you—climbing an invisible staircase to the attic. According to one report, the legend was boosted after a police search dog was called in one night because of a suspected burglar. The dog got spooked for some reason and refused to go near the attic.

And that's not the end of ghostly presences near Steilacoom. Psychiatric hospitals are always good for spooky stories, and there are plenty surrounding the town's Western State Hospital. The facility, originally known as the Insane Asylum of Washington Territory, opened in 1871 on the grounds of what had been Fort Steilacoom in suburban Lakewood. The original facility housed a grand total of fifteen male and six female patients; today, Western State now accommodates about eight hundred.

The old hospital's graveyard is now part of nearby Fort Steilacoom Park. Patients who died at the mental facility between 1876 and 1953—about 3,200 according to the hospital's records—were buried in graves marked only with a numbered headstone. This was according to state law, the reasoning being that identification as a mentally ill person could stigmatize that person's family. However, according to a 2009 *Seattle Times* article by Sharon Pian Chan, then-Governor Gary Locke overturned the law in 2004, and today a volunteer group is working to identify the bodies in all of the graves by name.

The vast number of Western State's unmarked graves has led to persistent rumors about the ghostly presence of the facility's mentally disturbed patients. Some people have speculated that the spirits of these forgotten people still wander the area. Allegedly, staff members have also reported witnessing creepy stuff such as elevators operating on their own, mysterious shadows moving down brightly lit hallways, and the inexplicable sounds of water running.

All of these stories are not the end of the ghostly tales that persist in the Tacoma area. Way back in 1899, the September 28 edition of the *Seattle Daily Times* carried a front-page story simply headlined: A MURDER.

The article reports that a forty-five-year-old Frenchman, Albert Michaud, was arrested for the shooting of his ex-wife, who had remarried and become Mrs. Julia Amber. It further reported that the murder was "the outgrowth of jealous rage and persecution on his part extending over a period of seven years."

This tragic event was by no means the only altercation the two had experienced. Three years before the fatal incident, Michaud had confronted his ex-wife at the hospital where she worked. He shot both her and himself, though not fatally. Michaud spent three years in the penitentiary for the crime, during which time he learned his wife had divorced him and remarried a man named Amber.

After his release, the felon returned to Tacoma and walked into the Ambers' home. Their daughter was at a neighbor's on an errand at the time, and John Amber, the husband, was not due home for another ten minutes. When she saw her vengeful ex-husband, Mrs. Amber fled out the back door as Michaud fired a .45 revolver at her. She got as far as the street before she fell, and Michaud shot her three times at such close range that her clothing caught fire.

The killer then tried to shoot himself, but the gun jammed. Several men followed in pursuit, and he was captured a short distance away. "He was drunk," the *Daily Times* reported, "and so excited he could not place a cartridge in the revolver with which to shoot himself, that being his manifest intention. A number of angry men soon gathered and began to talk of lynching."

But they refrained, and Michaud was jailed. Convicted of murder, he was hung in 1890 in the county courthouse on Tacoma Avenue South. According to legend, Michaud's hair had gone from jet-black to white just in the year of his incarceration. Also according to legend, a forlorn ghost still haunts the neighborhood near the Amber household, the scene of the murder. It's said that Julia roams the streets nearby, hoping that her tragic story can be completed and her spirit laid to rest.

And then there's the story of Eben Boyce, another story that started with a domestic dispute and ended when a woman's death resulted in another legend of otherworldly visitors. It seems that Boyce murdered his estranged wife, who had been working in a Tacoma restaurant in August 1901. The jealous and deranged Boyce tracked her down and, when he found her, killed her with a pistol. He was tried, convicted, and sentenced to death. Portland's *Sunday Oregonian* newspaper commented:

> [Boyce was] well known to Portland play-
> goers and to professional musicians, he
> having played the cornet at various places
> of amusement for nearly four years prior to
> the beginning of the Spanish-American War.
> . . . Many Portlanders think the newspapers
> of Tacoma were rather severe on the doomed
> man, who was never known here as an opium
> fiend or drinker of wood alcohol. He often
> went on sprees, and was very eccentric, but
> his friends cannot believe that he committed in
> cold blood the crime for which he was executed.

They argued instead that he was insane and that his sentence should have been commuted to life in prison. But their pleas were in vain, and Boyce was, like Michaud, hung in the county courthouse.

Not surprisingly, these two sensational murders of the ex-wives of Albert Michaud and Eben Boyce have become fertile ground for ghost stories—stories about dead men who still haunt the place where they were executed. Specifically, the spirits of these two bad men are said to still be seen wandering the halls of what is now known as the County-City Building of Tacoma and Pierce County. And, so they say, the old guys are looking pretty murderous. . . .

THORNEWOOD CASTLE

Located on American Lake in Lakewood, a suburb of Tacoma, Thornewood Castle is a luxury bed-and-breakfast, so beautiful and historically important that it is on the National Register of Historic Places. It's also Tacoma's best-known haunted mansion. Coincidence? You be the judge.

Thornewood Castle is an amazing place. It was built by one of the region's most prominent citizens in his day, banker and businessman Chester Thorne and his wife, Anna. The Thornes spent four years building the place and completed it in 1911. It boasted extensive gardens (originally on one hundred acres, though only about forty are still part of the property). The building itself is three stories high and totals about thirty thousand square feet, with fifty-four rooms, including twenty-eight bedrooms and twenty-two baths.

When it was first occupied, the estate required over two dozen full-time gardeners and an indoor staff of about forty. During this period, US presidents Theodore Roosevelt and William Howard Taft were just two of Thornewood's honored guests. The mansion's lord and master continued to act his role as a civic leader, meanwhile, heading the National Bank of Tacoma and helping to create the still-thriving Port of Tacoma. He was also an activist for the preservation of wilderness land, perhaps inspired by his guest Teddy Roosevelt's enthusiasm for the outdoors. To this end, Thorne was a key figure in the creation of Mount Rainier National Park.

But there's more to Thornewood than its place in history. It's also said that the mansion is thoroughly haunted by spirits—and not all of them are friendly spirits.

The establishment's current owners, Deanna and Wayne Robinson, claim that strange things have happened there so often that their daughter, as well as some of their employees, won't spend time in the castle alone. Glass bowls spontaneously shatter. Books move. Footsteps and distant unexplained voices and smells are apparent.

One guest reported a chilling incident while staying in the bridal suite. The air suddenly turned cold although all the windows were closed. Sensing movement, the guest saw the sheer curtain covering the closet door billow out. As she watched in terror, a pale, tall, thin man emerged from the closet. She later reported that he had dark hair and long sideburns, was apparently in his early thirties, and was dressed in slacks, a loose white shirt, and a black vest. He walked around the foot of the bed, sat down in a chair, looked directly at the woman, and then slowly vanished.

And that's hardly all of the goings-on at Thornewood Castle. It seems that lightbulbs unscrew themselves in what once was the gentlemen's parlor. Deanna Robinson says she got tired of screwing the bulbs back in and chastised one of the resident spirits: the original owner, who was the ghost she suspected was annoying her. The mischief stopped completely for two weeks after that, she says, and now only comes back periodically, if the spirit is angry or pleased about something.

The people making these reports include Robinson, the building's current gardener, and other employees and guests. They have repeatedly reported that Chester is usually the one responsible for the lightbulb gag and other forms of mischief. According to legend, he's also been seen on Thornewood's lawn, dressed in a brown riding suit. And a Robinson family friend claims that she once felt a strange presence while she was inside the house. When she turned around, there was Chester, dressed in the same brown suit. He allegedly asked her what she was doing and then vanished.

Meanwhile, Anna can be spotted sitting in the window seat or reflected in the mirror of her room. According to some guests, they have seen her at the same window as they walked in the garden. (Today, Anna's room is the bridal suite. Stay there at your own risk, honeymooners.)

Chester and Anna Thorne aren't the only ghosts who allegedly haunt the place. Another is the spirit of their son-in-law, Cadwallader Colden Corse. (Is that a great name or what?) Cadwallader was apparently gravely injured in an accident in Thornewood's gun closet—possibly a suicide attempt. (Some sources say the accident actually happened in a bathroom under the main staircase.)

In any case, Cadwallader and the Thornes' daughter, Anita, divorced after he recovered from his injury, and it's said that today his spirit can be seen walking around the castle. No word on whether or not his ghost is horribly disfigured from the accident.

Cadwallader's presence and all of the other reports of paranormal activity at the castle, naturally, have over the years attracted the attention of several organizations that specialize in investigating the unknown. After one such expedition, paranormal researchers reported that they could definitely hear a child singing.

One possible explanation for the presence of children in the mansion is that the spirit is the Thornes' daughter, Anita, trapped in time as a youngster. Another possible explanation involves persistent reports of a child-size spirit that is sometimes spotted standing alone on the shore of nearby American Lake. It's said that this is the ghost of a former owner's grandchild—a child who had tragically drowned in the lake.

Chester Thorne died in 1927. After that, his wife maintained the house, served on Chester's bank's board of directors, and oversaw the family's philanthropic work. Their daughter apparently also continued to live in the mansion.

There's one more fascinating detail about the possible haunting of Thornewood Castle. This story concerns the mansion's construction crew, which included a group of Native Americans hired by Thorne. While working on the mansion's basement and foundation, they hung a number of so-called wishbone sticks on the floor joists. The intent was to provide protection to the construction workers from evil spirits, protect the Thornes from any evil spirits that might come in the future, and bring good fortune to the house in general.

Considering the sad fate of Cadwallader and others, the evil spirits may have been able to elude this protective shield. Perhaps because of this continued need for protection, in 2004 two Native Americans performed a "smudge ceremony" to renew the wishbone sticks' powers. The pair who performed this ceremony explained about the ritual:

> White sage and cedar are burned and the smoke then fanned over the object with eagle and hawk feathers. This is to cleanse, purify and bless objects, homes and people. It works to lift and dispel negativity and darkness, similar to lifting a burr off an animal's fur. In the same manner, we as humans sometimes allow and engage depression, negative thoughts, despair and the weight of daily rigor to stick to us and weigh us down. This ceremony helps us to actively dislodge these encumbrances and frees us to once again allow the positive forces and light to renew our spirit.

Today, the Robinsons say they have no intention of trying to dislodge any of their otherworldly guests. Deanna Robinson told a *Seattle Times* reporter, "We don't want anything changed here. Whatever energy is here, we want it just the way it is."

ROSE RED

For years, Thornewood has been a favorite vacation destination. Not surprisingly, a major portion of its fans are attracted by its reputation for the otherworldly. And one factor in particular has added greatly to its reputation for mystery: the mansion's contribution to the world of spooky cinema.

Thornewood Castle was the location for the filming of *Rose Red,* a six-hour miniseries based on a script by horror-meister Stephen King and broadcast in 2002.

King's unnerving story told the tale of Joyce Reardon, a parapsychologist from "Beaumont University" (a thoroughly fictional institution). As the story opens, she and her team of researchers set out to investigate a series of inexplicable murders in a haunted building.

This Seattle mansion was supposedly located on the corner of 7th Avenue and Spring Street in downtown Seattle. However, Thornewood Castle was the real-life shooting location for this fictional Seattle mansion.

So far, not so strange—plenty of movies are set in one place but actually shot in another. What made this production notable was the shocking number of people who thought that (a) the story was real and (b) there was a real haunted mansion in Seattle.

The miniseries' producers enthusiastically fanned these fans' credulity with a massive marketing campaign. The moviemakers did this in part by creating a fake website credited to the thoroughly bogus "Beaumont University." They also produced a "mockumentary," a fake documentary about the mansion's hauntings that was aired prior to the mini-series. They even put together a book, *The Diary of Ellen Rimbauer,* that was purportedly written by one of the mansion's original owners. The book, which became a bestseller, was in fact written by respected thriller writer

Ridley Pearson. Quoted in a *Tacoma News Tribune* article in 2003, Pearson commented that many people didn't realize that the book was fiction: "And to this day we get many, many letters from people who are actually convinced that it is Ellen Rimbauer's diary, and asking where the house is. People really bought into the joke."

Nor, by any means, were King and Pearson the only recipients of such letters. Immediately after the airing of the show, Seattle historians and guides were inundated by requests for information. Staff members at the Klondike Gold Rush National Historical Park, in Pioneer Square near the alleged location of the house, reported that in the wake of *Rose Red* they were regularly approached by visitors hoping to visit the haunted mansion. Meanwhile, Historylink.org, a website of Washington State history founded by the late Walter Crowley, began receiving a massive influx of letters and emails, similarly asking where in Seattle the mansion could be found. A selection of these emails can be found on the Historylink site. One sample, complete with creative spelling and punctuation, asks:

> why does your sight say that Rose Red is fictional
> when it is an actural occurance . . . ? . . . also
> where can I obtain a clear picture of John and Ellen
> Rimbauer . . . ? where can I find more information
> on this subject . . . I have already seen the sight
> at Baumont university but that is limited where
> can I find more such as newspaper clippings from
> the actual city where Rose Red is . . . etc. . . . and
> pictures and other missing excerpts that dr. joyce
> reardon withheld from the public. . . . ?

Spooky indeed. And here's another strange twist to the story: Actor David Dukes, who played Professor Carl Miller, died while filming the movie. Dukes, who was only fifty-five, suffered a fatal heart attack while playing tennis. His widow, novelist Carole Muske-Dukes, carried on a lengthy battle over what she saw as the mishandling by the Pierce County medical examiner of his autopsy and subsequent embalming. Muske-Dukes told the *Seattle Post-Intelligencer*, "This medical examiner created a terrible second loss. It's like a second death." Could Dukes's tragic and untimely demise have added to Thornewood's reputation for sad and eerie events?

Chapter 6

The Kitsap Peninsula and Olympia, the State Capital

The Kitsap Peninsula, in Pierce County, is a ferry ride across Puget Sound from Seattle, and it is separated from the rest of the Olympic Peninsula (the part of the state that is farther to the west, toward the Pacific) by a narrow passage called Hood Canal. The peninsula's biggest city, Bremerton, is the site of a major military facility, the US Navy's Puget Sound Naval Shipyard.

The setting of the Kitsap Peninsula—a narrow area of low-lying land almost completely surrounded by salt water—makes it an attractive place for all those who love the water's edge. It's a relatively small area of land, but nonetheless has some 230 miles of saltwater shoreline.

South of the Kitsap Peninsula, meanwhile, is Thurston County, the site of Washington State's capital, Olympia. Before the arrival of white settlers, the region around Olympia was called Cheet-woot ("place of black bears"), and it was an important gathering ground for the several Indian tribes in the area, including the Nisqually, Duwamish, and Squaxin peoples. Could Thurston County and the Kitsap Peninsula also be the site of strange and otherworldly apparitions?

STARVATION HEIGHTS

Choosing the strangest, creepiest, and spookiest episode in Washington's history? That would be a tough assignment.

But the story of Starvation Heights, in the small town of Olalla on the Kitsap Peninsula, surely ranks in the top tier. The specter of death surrounding it, some say, continues to this day—personified, so to speak, by the spirits of people who died there. The source of this eerie feeling? A ruthless and murderous con artist and the clinic she founded to impose a horrific "health" regimen on the wealthy but gullible.

This was Starvation Heights, the nickname given to a notorious sanitarium in the first decade of the twentieth century. Linda Burfield Hazzard, the establishment's owner and operator, convinced a number of desperately ill people that they could regain their health by eating only a thin vegetable soup for months at a time. This "cure" was offered mainly to people for—you guessed it—a considerable fee.

Not surprisingly, patient after patient died. The exact number of deaths is unknown, but it was at least a dozen and perhaps as many as forty. After each one, Hazzard and her husband, having obtained (or forged) the power of attorney over a victim, cleaned out the hapless victim's bank accounts. Author Gregg Olsen, who wrote a well-respected book about the Hazzards, told a *Kitsap Sun* reporter in 2011 that the building where the Hazzards carried out their scheme was "the most murderous house in Washington history."

Linda Hazzard, born in Minnesota in 1867, began touting her fabulous cure while barely out of her teens. It focused on ridding the body of "impure blood" through extreme purging. The Hazzard method included starvation, painful daily enemas that lasted hours and used up to twelve quarts of water, and regular massages, during which she beat her fists against the patients while urging them to "Eliminate! Eliminate!"

Hazzard apparently caused her first death while still in Minnesota. Soon thereafter, law enforcement made the curious discovery that her patient's jewelry had gone missing. However, the police investigators didn't have enough evidence of wrongdoing to prosecute.

In 1906, the con artist and her ex-felon husband, Sam Hazzard, moved to a forty-acre spread in Olalla, planning to build a sanitarium. "Doctor" Hazzard soon became a charismatic celebrity in the Pacific Northwest, attracting many members of Seattle's elite business and social circles. Olsen comments, "If she walked into a room, she'd take charge of it. If she was alive today, she'd be a big star."

In 1908, Daisey Haglund, suffering from stomach cancer, became the first person in Washington to die under Hazzard's supervision. A curious footnote: Daisey's young son, Ivar Haglund, grew up to become a much-loved Seattle restaurateur. By feeding the public his fish and chips, Ivar was in a very real sense the opposite of Linda Hazzard.

Several more deaths followed, and public concern about Starvation Heights began to grow. Nonetheless, patients continued to enlist Hazzard's "help." Authorities tried to stop her, especially after the death of magazine publisher Lewis Ellsworth Rader. The five-foot-eleven Rader weighed less than a hundred pounds when he died. But Hazzard was allowed to continue because her patients sought her out willingly.

Although in many cases the residents of Starvation Heights arrived willingly, they were not always eager to stay. Locals sometimes saw dazed and delirious patients in town, begging for food or help. But the locals did little to stop Hazzard. She was educated and wealthy, and the people of Olalla, most of them poor immigrants, trusted that she knew best.

The end came with the arrival of Dora and Claire Williamson, a pair of wealthy British sisters. Concerned because she couldn't contact them, the sisters' childhood nanny paid a visit. Hazzard informed her that Claire had fallen fatally ill and that Dora was unable to leave because the treatment could not stop.

The nanny informed the British vice-consul in Tacoma, he pressured Kitsap County authorities, and Hazzard was arrested in 1911. A headline in the *Tacoma Daily News* read, "Officials Expect to Expose Starvation Atrocities: Dr. Hazzard Depicted as Fiend."

During her trial, Hazzard had the support of many loyal clients. One was Johan Ivar Haglund, who credited Hazzard with having eased his wife Daisey's condition as she died. But the jury convicted her of manslaughter, and two more patients died while Hazzard awaited sentencing. She served two years in the state penitentiary, after which she and Sam fled to New Zealand.

In 1920, however, she returned to Olalla, determined to establish a "school of health" and continuing to tout her methods until 1938, when she died of—wait for it—a fasting cure.

As of 2013, the one-hundred-bed dormitory at Starvation Heights still stood, as did the moldering remains of the Hazzards' cottage. The *Kitsap Sun* reporter commented, "The house still has a few remnants of the Hazzard household. The hook used to boil kettles for enemas still juts from the fireplace. The original bathtub—the one Hazzard used for autopsies—still sits in the bathroom."

Not surprisingly, Starvation Heights has become a magnet for tales of the otherworldly—including stories about the skeletal ghosts of former patients, begging for help after death just as they did in life.

PORT GAMBLE

At the far northern tip of the Kitsap Peninsula, there's the picturesque little town of Port Gamble. PG, as it's called, has more than its share of buildings that have been preserved and restored to their original Victorian charm—so many, in fact, that the entire town is a National Historic Landmark.

Yes, Port Gamble is darling—but it's also considered by many to be one of the most densely haunted places in the state. One estimate suggests that at least half the buildings there house a variety of spine-chilling presences. As a whole, the town has such a reputation as a hotbed of hauntings that it hosts an annual Port Gamble Ghost Conference.

The town's most imposing mansion, the Walker-Ames House, highlights the contrast between its picturesque beauty and its reputation for the otherworldly. In 2011, *Kitsap Herald* reporter Erin Jennings noted this when she wrote, "The grand staircase, stained glass windows and ornate woodwork in the home [are] juxtaposed with peeling wallpaper, a stained bathtub and a basement that could frighten Stephen King."

Port Gamble wasn't always so spooky. It started life as a thriving lumbering community, founded in 1851 as a town for the Puget Sound Mill Company. As the lumber industry in the Pacific Northwest diminished, so did the fortunes of Port Gamble, and in 1995 the mill closed down (but not before earning the honor of being the longest continuously operating mill in America).

The mill closure was bad news for the local economy, although the town has bounced back somewhat thanks to the flocks of tourists who visit and the hard work of the residents who have preserved and restored their town to its original Victorian beauty.

In the meantime, it seems, the ghosts never left.

Take the aforementioned Walker-Ames House, built by an early mill superintendent, Cyrus Walker, and occupied after his retirement by his successor (and son-in-law) Edwin Ames. Reported otherworldly experiences there have ranged from full-bodied apparitions to less definite (but just as spooky) feelings of cold dread.

Other reports about the uninhabited building include frequent sightings of three small, ghostly children and their nanny through an upstairs window; the spirit of a house-keeper that follows guests around; a man lingering in the servants' hallways; and a mysterious, old-fashioned lady in the parlor.

Furthermore, there's apparently a spirit in the basement who enjoys touching women and pulling their hair. The story goes that this is the ghost of a mentally ill boy who once lived in the house. His mother kept him locked in the basement, so it's no surprise that he isn't fond of females.

There have also been reports that the Walker-Ames House's attic light turns itself on and off in the otherwise empty building. Cold spots, inexplicable flowery scents, and areas that create a feeling of dread or sadness are also often reported. Fully charged camera and cell phone batteries have been said to drain completely if they're brought into the basement.

But wait—there's more! A panel beneath the staircase, covering a hidden storage space, was at one point found mysteriously dislodged. Strangely, there was only one door handle—on the inside—so when it was closed there was no way to reopen it. Did it once house something eerie that needed a door handle to get out, but not in?

Elsewhere in PG, you can find plenty of other stories about spooky occurrences. Take, for instance, the Thompson House, so named for the family that lived there for nearly a century. Port Gamble's town manager, Shana Smith, lives there now and says she's a believer, having heard the very late Mr. Thompson's footsteps on the stairs. And then there's the building that now serves as the town's community center but was once its morgue. A number of witnesses have reported hearing voices and footsteps on the floor above them—when no one was there.

Then there's Mike's Four Star BBQ. Back when Mike's was a service station, a man named Pete Orbea reports that he was alone, working in the back room, when he saw a tool fly six feet in the air, bang against the wall, and crash to the ground.

Furthermore, according to legend a plumber fixing some pipes underneath one of the town's houses found an antique doll and took it away with him. He later discovered that he'd lost his cell phone. Sensing that the two incidents were connected somehow, he returned the doll to its original location—and came home to find his cell phone sitting on the front porch, out in the open where he couldn't have missed seeing it earlier.

Still another story about the town: It's alleged that a strange voice has been caught on tape—that of Gustave Englebrecht, an early settler who was killed by Native Americans in 1856.

The many aficionados of paranormal phenomena who visit Port Gamble are not the only ones who appreciate the town. The film industry has also taken advantage of its combination of placid beauty and all things creepy.

Specifically, Port Gamble was both the setting and the shooting location for the horror-comedy film *ZMD: Zombies of Mass Destruction,* shot in 2009 and released the following year. In an article on the shooting, a writer for the *Kitsap Herald* commented, "Port Gamble is almost a movie set in itself. The silence of the old logging town is deafening late at night. The idyllic, archaic architecture stands stoic and spooky against a backdrop of the night sky looming above an empty town. As the fog sets in, it doesn't take much of a stretch to imagine this place really could've been recently evacuated and quarantined in the aftermath [of] a zombie attack."

Apparently, the film's crew felt the strange vibes while they were in town. Crewmembers using the Walker-Ames home as a backdrop were reportedly reluctant to go into the basement alone, and one female worker apparently fell afoul of the basement lurker. She stated that while she was down there alone, someone grabbed her and left a bruise in the shape of a handprint on her leg.

Maybe the lesson to be learned from Port Gamble's combination of beauty and spine-tingling ghosts is: It's just a short hop from charm to harm. . . .

OLYMPIA

What can you say about a college that has as its athletic mascot the geoduck, a shellfish that looks like a clam on steroids? You say: That must be the Evergreen State College in the state capital of Olympia.

As you can guess, Evergreen is an alternative educational facility that prides itself on innovation and a high quirkiness quotient. (Incidentally, the name of its noble bivalve of a mascot is pronounced "gooey-duck." Say it correctly and impress your friends!)

But we digress. Back to ghosts: In 2009, Evergreen student Ty Rosenow wrote a paper as a school project: "Myths Unveiled: The Social History of the Evergreen State College." Among the topics the paper covers are several ghostly campus legends. One of these is a persistent belief that a ghost inhabits the school's library building. People have allegedly spotted the spirit in the cafeteria, basement, periodicals section, main stacks on the third floor, and other rooms.

Rosenow also mentions a tale about the Churchman family, who lived on twenty-two wooded acres that are now part of the Evergreen campus. Their house, which still stands, came with a resident spirit when it was incorporated into Evergreen's land. The spirit was pretty benign and got up to typical hijinks, such as opening and closing doors, turning lights on and off, and running faucets.

The spirit, who was a man, was seen at the window, but when the family went outside to investigate he had disappeared. They also reported that their dogs would periodically go crazy, running around and barking wildly—something they didn't do unless a stranger was present, which didn't appear to be the case. Also, neighbors periodically heard music coming from the house—rock and roll, which was definitely not to the Churchmans' taste. And on their last night there, the family was awakened by the inexplicable sound of chains dropping on the floor.

Reporter Joyce Nelson of the *Daily Olympian* wrote about the case in 1968, when the property was sold to the state. Nelson wrote, "Even if you're not gullible about ghosts it's hard to shake the shivers when you think that in the West Olympia woods may prowl a real, live ghost—in a manner of speaking." She explains this by reprinting a letter the Churchman family wrote to future Evergreen students:

> We, the Churchman family of the Lewis Road, west of Olympia, wish to leave a legacy to The Evergreen State College, which will occupy the land we have called home for the last ten years.
>
> We have left now, after a reluctant sale of our home. . . .We leave behind us one small member of your family whom we find it impossible to move. We leave you our household guest.
>
> He came to us about four years ago and his presence has been a part of our lives since the day he entered our home unannounced. He is often heard walking about the house and gravel paths and he is often seen and heard opening the doors of the home and other buildings. He seems to be quite at home and comes at all hours of the day and night. He has never attempted to harm any member of the family.
>
> Not only are we used to his comings and goings, but the family dogs now ignore him though he is heard walking within a few feet of them. Sometimes they will look when he opens a door but never make a fuss about it.
>
> We wonder why he chose our home. Was there something here we never understood?
>
> We are going to miss him but we feel our friend will be a good member of the new college. We wonder which group of students he will choose for his new companions when the school is finished and

occupied. We hope you will be kind to him, future students, and accept him as we have. Treat him well. He is our legacy to you.

The library ghost and that of the Churchman house seem harmless enough. But a more somber, uncanny story revolves around a real-life monster: the notorious serial killer Ted Bundy, who assaulted and murdered at least thirty women in the 1970s. Rosenow quotes an unnamed female student whose mother had been a friend of Donna Gail Manson, who in 1974 became one of Bundy's victims. The student related, "I was in the dormitory kitchen when I felt a hand patting me on my right shoulder. That was when I turned around and saw Donna Gail Manson's ghost. The ghost said, 'Do I know your mother?' and I said 'Yeah,' and began to point to a picture I had handy with me." This picture was in the student's notebook. The ghost took one look at it—and disappeared.

Plenty of other places in Olympia besides the Evergreen campus have reported ghosts over the years. Among these are the Capitol House Apartments on Sherman Street, which once was a hospital; the historic Bigelow House on Glass Avenue, named for early Olympia lawyer Daniel R. Bigelow and his family; another old house, the McCleary Mansion; the Forest Memorial Gardens Cemetery; the fourth floor of Avanti High School on Legion Way; the Old Tumwater Brewery; and the Old Main building at St. Martin's University.

But don't forget a more famous place that deserves at least an honorary mention: the Governor's Mansion.

Okay, so strictly speaking the mansion is not haunted—but there was something that caused shivers to travel up some people's spines: a bat infestation. In 1997, shortly after moving into the mansion, then-governor Gary Locke, his wife, and their infant daughter were forced to relocate temporarily while the bats—at least a dozen of them—were captured.

The first inkling of the bats' presence came when the first family's two cats were found playing with one in the mansion's laundry room. But the scariest incident was when the governor spotted a bat late one night. It circled above baby Emily's crib as Locke changed her diaper. Locke chased the bat into the mansion's ballroom and slammed the door.

That episode convinced government officials—and the Lockes themselves—that they needed to move out. The governor and his family took up residence in a nearby private home and were vaccinated against rabies as a precaution, as bat teeth are so small that it is possible for humans to be bitten and not notice it. Locke later went on to serve as the US Secretary of Commerce and ambassador to China, so presumably he and his family remained unbitten by the creepy flying creatures.

TENINO

South of Olympia is the small town of Tenino. Today, Tenino is best known to history geeks for the brief national fame it earned during the Great Depression of the 1930s, when banks all across America were forced to close. Following the collapse of the Citizens Bank of Tenino, the town's Chamber of Commerce came up with a novel plan to relieve the resulting critical shortage of money in the region.

The solution? Wooden money. This currency was scrip that people could use temporarily in the town; in exchange, depositors agreed to give the chamber up to 25 percent of their bank account balances at a future date. The new form of money was printed frugally, using something Tenino had in abundance: spruce or cedar scraps, called slice wood, left over from the operations of the region's sawmills.

Tenino's wooden money scheme became the object of considerable publicity, including national newspapers and radio broadcasts—even a mention in the *Congressional Record*, during a Senate debate on possible measures to rebuild the nation's economy.

In all, eight issues of wooden money were printed in 1932 and 1933. A total of $10,308 (in denominations of 25 cents, 50 cents, $1, $5, and $10) went into circulation, although the chamber redeemed only $40. Most of the scraps of wood became collector's items. The idea of wooden money was so novel that it attracted a number of tourists to remote little Tenino. These visitors were eager to buy the scrip as souvenirs. Because they paid the residents of Tenino in cash, it made the scrip experiment a modestly profitable venture for the town.

Tenino's wooden money came from what was then a major factor in the region's economy: a thriving lumber industry. But Tenino's nickname, the Stone City, reflects another aspect of that early economy: nearby limestone quarries, abundant sources of building material in the early decades of the region's settlement.

That's a clear enough explanation of the town's nickname. But the origin of Tenino's actual name—now, that's a real source of mystery. Does it mean "a branch in the trail" or "meeting place" in the Chinook language, the common jargon used by many Native American tribes in the area? Does it stem from a railway locomotive with the numbers 10-9-0? Did the name migrate somehow up from Oregon, where it was used to collectively refer to several bands of Warm Springs Indians, or from streets of the same name in towns as far away as Colorado and Texas? All of these have been put forward as possible explanations, but the issue has never been settled.

In any case, whatever lies behind the mystery of Tenino's name, there are other mysteries to be found in the town. The most prominent of these is the tale of Uncle Charlie Jackson, his dog Wolf, and a creepy photo of the house they once lived in.

The story about Charlie's ghost started in 1979, when a real estate broker began getting ready to sell the decrepit, 1880s-vintage house that Jackson had built and lived in until his death in the 1930s. Harry R. Bay of the *Tenino Daily Chronicle* wrote in 1979 that taking photos of the place was the beginning of a strange journey: "When Janet Cobb of Tenino Realty knelt by the frame two-story house to snap pictures, she never dreamed [that] she was coming face-to-face with the unexplained."

One of the spots she recorded that day was the entrance to a crawlspace. As she knelt to take a snap, she felt something bump against her, although there were no people or animals nearby. Her camera was a Polaroid Instamatic, so she could tell right away that the picture was not a good one. Not thinking that the bump she felt was anything much, she just snapped another in the same spot.

When Cobb got back to her office, however, she looked more closely at the pictures she had taken. Most of them were not unusual, but she noticed that the second photo of the crawlspace entrance was very odd indeed. She told Bay, "Prior to shooting the first picture, something bumped me, but no animal or person was in sight. The second picture contained the eerie image of a man's face and a dog's head."

The strange image was nothing more than a minor puzzle to Cobb and her colleagues at the real estate office. But the next month, by coincidence, a Tenino native named Harold Cavin came into the office asking to see about properties. He happened to notice the photo and, as he told Bay, he "almost had a heart attack."

According to Cavin, the picture bore images of Jackson and his dog.

Soon after, when the mayor of nearby Bucoda heard about the ghostly images, he searched through his files and found a photo of Jackson and his wife taken about 1895. The mayor told reporter Bay, "I was astonished with the resemblances between the picture of Charles Jackson and the image of a man's face on the photo Janet Cobb snapped."

The incident had a special meaning for Cavin. He knew Jackson well, calling him Uncle Charlie, although Jackson was actually his great-great-uncle. As a boy, Cavin had taken fiddle lessons from him (Jackson often performed at local dances) and frequently played with his dog, Wolf.

So the photos immediately resonated with Cavin. He quickly came to the realization that he had to find a way to preserve Jackson's home. Cavin told Bay, "I believe those images on that picture were a message to me to save the house."

So Cavin bought a two-acre parcel of land adjoining the property and, hoping to preserve it as a historical monument, tried to have the house moved about four hundred yards onto his property. He was not successful, however, and the building was burned down to make way for a new structure.

Officially, the eerie story of the Tenino haunting is closed. Nonetheless, as many people interested in the supernatural point out, it's not always easy to get rid of ghosts—and some locals say that the spirits of Uncle Charlie and Wolf still roam the property where they once lived.

Chapter 7

Olympic Peninsula: From *Twilight* to Real Crime and Back

No look at Washington State's haunted places would be complete without a survey of the Olympic Peninsula, the far northwest section of the state.

Heavily forested and one of the rainiest parts of the world, the interior of the peninsula is also a forbidding place that can produce more than its share of frightening stories. Out on the coastline that snakes around it, meanwhile, you can find some tales that are equally spine-tingling.

FORKS

The little town of Forks, a little ways inland from the coastal Quileute Indian Reservation, was for years a quiet, economically depressed logging center. But Forks has skyrocketed into prosperity and the pop-culture stratosphere thanks to one phenomenon: the *Twilight* series.

Okay, so it's not strictly a ghostly region. But it's still pretty spooky—and apparently chock-full of various types of the undead.

It's not hard to see why author Stephenie Meyer set her wildly popular novels about vampires and humans in Forks. The town is widely known as one of the wettest spots in the United States, with an average rainfall of 121 inches and an average snowfall of 11 inches every year.

Its surroundings—deep, dark forests and the wild Pacific coast to the west—only add to the place's general sense of gloom.

Thanks to Meyer's books—not to mention the movies that have followed—Forks has become a must-see destination for droves of vampire lovers, who make pilgrimages from all over the world to see the real-life world of *Twilight*. (The fact that the movies weren't filmed there doesn't seem to stop them.) As you'd expect, the fortunes of Forks residents have changed dramatically, and local businesses have made a strong effort to capitalize on the town's sudden fame.

So the *Twilight* theme and references to its characters are evident everywhere. Take the Miller Tree Inn Bed and Breakfast, which, as its website states, "was appointed as the Cullen House by the Tourism Board and plays the part with messages from the 'Twilight' character Esme for visitors." The Forks Tourism Office offers information on such activities as haunted trail hikes and guided tours of *Twilight*-related high points. (Don't miss the Dazzled by Twilight gift shop or the parking spot reserved for "Dr. Cullen" at the Forks Community Hospital. And if you have to ask who Dr. Cullen is, you probably don't need to take the tour.) Furthermore, if you head west to the coast, you can stop at La Push, home of *Twilight*'s werewolf community.

Beyond the whole *Twilight* thing, the Forks region has many other close connections with the supernatural—or at least the super-spooky.

For example, you can include in the latter category the various ghost forests in the region—that is, forest areas that have died due to earthquakes or other disasters, leaving only vast tracts of dead trees behind. And then there are the many breathtakingly beautiful but rather eerie places within Olympic National Park.

One of these is Lake Crescent. As one of the state's most prominent hiking organizations, the Washington Trails Association, puts it, "Lake Crescent has secrets. At first glance, its shimmering clear water appears to reveal everything. But its depths plunge to a pitch black 624 feet or more, and the lake is known for rarely giving up its dead."

Hiking in the Lake Crescent area—especially along the Spruce Railroad Trail—will conjure some of its many and genuinely creepy, ghostly mysteries.

In a 2001 article, *Seattle Post-Intelligencer* reporter Kristin Dizon commented, "In legend and lore, Lake Crescent is a living being, and sometimes a malicious one. Local tales say the Klallam Indians refused to cross the glacier-carved lake by canoe because evil spirits would snatch them to the icy depths. For years, locals suspected that the lake was bottomless. Some swore they'd spotted a sea monster in its azure ripples."

Lake Crescent is also the location of one of the strangest deaths in the state's history—and one that might have resulted in the ghosts of a murdered man and woman.

On July 3, 1929, Russell and Blanche Warren were driving from Port Angeles to their home near the Bogachiel River, west of Forks, planning to spend the Fourth of July with their boys, then twelve and fourteen. But the last time the couple was seen was a few miles from Lake Crescent. They probably plunged into the lake while traveling US 101, which hugs the lakeshore and was then barely wide enough at times for two cars to pass.

Their disappearance was, Dizon notes, an enduring mystery: "Did their car careen off the dirt and gravel road into the depths of azure Lake Crescent, a cold, clear grave entombing them? Was it a simple accident on a curve taken too fast, or a drowsy driver at the helm, as most thought? Or had something more sinister happened—a spat between spouses grappling over the steering wheel? A murder? A deliberate disappearance?"

The local authorities dredged the lake for evidence and sent divers down. But no clues to the mystery turned up until early in the twenty-first century. Volunteer divers, long intrigued by the mystery, turned up several items, including a tire pump and a rusted car step. Then in 2002, they spotted what they believed to be the Warrens' 1927 Chevrolet in forty-five feet of water.

Working with these clues, the volunteer divers were able to pinpoint the car and reconstruct the accident.

Dizon noted, "Lake Crescent is a voracious tomb. She does not give up her dead easily. . . . No one knows how many lives have ended there, how many bodies are suspended in that crystal liquid."

And surely the strangest and most spine-tingling of these eerie stories is that of the Lady of the Lake. The tale hinges on a brutal murder and the bizarre way in which the victim's body was preserved.

Back in 1940, the body of Hallie Latham Illingworth, the victim in a three-year-old murder case, was found in Lake Crescent. Hallie was a barmaid at a nearby tavern and the wife of Monty Illingworth, a beer-truck driver and notorious ladies' man. It was apparently not a happy union; Hallie frequently came to work with bruises and black eyes, and just five months after the marriage, the local police intervened in a pre-dawn fight.

Then, in December 1937, Hallie vanished without a trace. Monty's story was that she ran off with a sailor from

Alaska. Not long after, Monty took off himself with another woman, and they settled in Long Beach, California. His story about Hallie rang false, but without a body the police had no evidence of wrongdoing.

Until the summer of 1940, that is, when two fishermen spotted something weird floating on the surface of the lake.

It was a body, wrapped in blankets and bound with heavy rope. It was Hallie. That would have been gruesome enough—but the local coroner and sheriff found something very strange indeed. . . .

The murdered woman's body was not bloated, as you'd expect of a body that had been in water for years. Nor was there any odor of decay. The corpse's skin was hard and waxy, and it was missing its fingertips and part of its face. Hallie's remains were also astonishingly light—only about fifty pounds, with a soap-like appearance and a strangely white coloring.

What had happened? An autopsy revealed that the corpse had undergone a process called saponification. Saponification is a common chemical process that involves converting fatty acids to soap. Sometimes, bodies also undergo saponification. In this case, the salt and calcium in the waters of Lake Crescent gradually turned Hallie's tissue into a soap-like substance called adipocere. At the same time, the lake's extremely cold water kept her body from decomposing. Hallie Illingsworth had become, essentially, a human-shaped, mummified bar of soap.

And, just like regular soap, a body that undergoes saponification becomes lighter than water. The ropes connecting weights to Hallie's body eventually decayed—and up she came.

Although the face and the tips of her toes and fingers were missing, Hallie could still be identified. Remnants of her distinctive dress and stockings remained, along with bits of her auburn hair. The clincher came thanks to the state attorney general's office, which confirmed her identity through dental records.

Monty Illingsworth was arrested in Long Beach later that year and extradited to Washington for trial. The trial, early in 1942, was so sensational that it competed with news of America's entry into World War II.

Illingsworth protested his innocence, but the evidence was compelling. After only four hours of deliberation, the jury found him guilty of second-degree murder, and he was sent to the Washington State Penitentiary in Walla Walla.

Not surprisingly, the grisly deaths in Lake Crescent of Russell and Blanche Warren and Hallie Illingsworth have led to a variety of ghostly legends. All three of them have been spotted roaming the lake's shores, perhaps looking for some kind of closure to their short lives and unhappy deaths. Now, you tell me that Lake Crescent doesn't have a creepy tale or two to relate. . . .

PORT TOWNSEND

The Olympic Peninsula town of Port Townsend is picturesque and sweet, and in recent years it's become a popular tourist stop. It's also the home of many an undead spirit.

Take one of the most prominent landmarks, Manresa Castle, in PT (as the town is called). The ornate thirty-room mansion was a fitting home for one of PT's biggest wheels and his wife, Charles and Kate Eisenbeis. Eisenbeis, a native of Prussia, was a prominent member of the early Port Townsend business community and the town's first mayor.

Eisenbeis built the home in 1892 and died in 1902. Not long afterward, his wife remarried and moved away. The castle remained uninhabited, except for a caretaker, until 1925, when a Seattle attorney purchased it as a retreat for nuns who taught school in Seattle. In 1927, the building was again sold, this time to a group of Jesuit priests for use as a training college. The Jesuits made several additions, including a chapel, a suite of personal quarters, and an elevator. They also renamed the place after Manresa, the Spanish town where the Jesuit order was founded.

Manresa Castle changed its identity again in 1968, when it became a hotel. Since then it has had several owners, all of whom have had a hand in renovating the mansion to its original Victorian splendor, complete with slightly ominous-looking turrets.

And, like any self-respecting Victorian-era mansion, the hotel also has its resident ghosts. According to legend, two people have died in the Manresa Castle: a Jesuit priest who hanged himself in Room 302 and a distraught woman who jumped from a window in Room 306. Some say the latter was a young Englishwoman named Kate who committed suicide after hearing that her true love had died at sea.

Rumor has it that a bartender in the hotel's bar made up the stories out of whole cloth as a way of entertaining guests. On the other hand, other tales relate that employees and guests alike have reported a variety of unusual and unexplainable activities, including being tugged on while they were sleeping, light fixtures swaying, objects moving on their own, and strange thumping and singing.

One Port Townsend resident who has a story to tell is Bruce Cowan, a schoolteacher and guitarist-singer who specializes in popular songs from the 1930s and 1940s. In an essay he wrote about his first appearance in the Manresa Castle's bar, Cowan recalled, "I've never put much stock in the stories of heartbroken maidens and suicidal priests. But I did see something that changed my mind about ghosts."

Between sets on that first gig, he relates, Cowan took a break, strolled around the Castle's formal gardens, and looked back at the ornate building. He wrote that it was a blustery night, with trees tossing in the moonlight and fallen leaves swirling around. As he returned, the heavy wooden door closed heavily behind him. The bartender had turned out the lights in the lounge to increase the intimate atmosphere, and the only illumination came from flickering candles on the tables. The bartender and a young couple were the only people in the lounge. She wore an old-fashioned hat and dress, and he was wearing a heavy wool Army uniform.

As Cowan got ready to play, the bartender called him over and said that the lady had requested a special song: a classic, "The Way You Look Tonight." It was one of Cowan's favorites too, so he smiled at the couple and started playing. As he did, the couple snuffed their cigarettes and moved closer together.

She leaned into him, their heads touching. When the song ended, the bartender signaled to "play it again, Bruce." This time the guitarist played it through without singing, and the couple sat up straight and faced each other. As they gazed into each other's eyes, they slowly rose to their feet. He kissed her tenderly, stood straight, and stepped back. As she leaned toward him, the soldier turned sharply and headed for the door—but he never got there. He crossed the room and just sort of . . . well, he just faded away. The woman watched him go, and then sank to her seat, looking toward the door, her eyes shining with tears.

Cowan was blinking himself, trying to understand what he'd just seen. He glanced at the bartender, who was calmly washing glasses, and then looked back at the woman. To his astonishment, she looked now to be in her eighties—still beautiful, but elderly. She was wearing an outfit that could have come straight out of the 1940s. The woman smiled at Cowan, her eyes brimming, and mouthed the words, "Thank you." When she stood, she was tall and straight-backed.

Cowan smiled in return, and the woman walked slowly through the doorway and up the stairs to the hotel. Amazed, Cowan looked at the bartender and said, "Did you see . . . that?" The bartender replied, "That lady? She comes in once a year, first Saturday in October. She always sits alone at that same table, has a Manhattan, and requests the same song. Then she walks out, and always leaves a nice tip."

The guitarist looked in his tip jar, which now held an odd-looking ten-dollar bill. He went over to the table—no ashtray, no cigarettes, and only a single glass. Cowan said to the bartender, "I thought I saw . . . uh, you've never seen anyone with her?" Then the bartender shook his head and said, "She said goodbye to her husband here during World War II. They'd been married a week and he had to leave that night. It was the last time she saw him. He died at Normandy."

The Manresa Castle is by no means Port Townsend's only haunted location. Downtown on Water Street, the owners of the 1889 Palace Hotel report so many paranormal activities that they keep a journal in which guests can record their experiences. Quoted in a 2009 article by Marcie Miller in the *Peninsula Daily News,* one entry in this book states, "I have never been more scared in my life than while I stayed at your hotel."

When it was built, the Palace's first floor housed a billiard parlor and saloon, the Townsend Tavern. Over the years it has housed a residential hotel, newspaper and railroad offices, a theater, a grocery store, a liquor store, a florist shop, and several restaurants.

There have been reports of bloodcurdling and inexplicable sounds of crying, perhaps the ghostly echoes of prostitutes—or perhaps, it has been ghoulishly suggested, babies that were buried in the basement. But the most commonly spotted apparition is the Lady in Blue, who is said to walk the halls on occasion. According to legend, she favors the second floor, which (as in so many buildings from that era) once served as a brothel—in this case, an establishment nicknamed "the Palace of Sweets." Perhaps, the present-day hotel's owners speculate, she is the same person whose portrait hangs in the hotel. Or perhaps she is one infamous lady of the night known as "Miss Claire" or another former resident. Whoever she is, people say, she appears to be a benign presence.

And then there's the imposing and lovely Ann Starrett Mansion on Clay Street, which also dates from 1889. It was built by a wealthy contractor, George E. Starrett, as a gift to his bride, Ann. Today, the building is a hotel and is reportedly haunted by a woman with red hair.

Quoted in the Miller piece, owner Edel Sokol noted that there have been plenty of stories over the years about the house. She commented, "A women's group this year reported seeing her floating down the stairs, and there is a no trespassing sign on those stairs."

Sokol added, however, that she is a skeptic in these matters: "If you want to see one, you'll see one. How can you dispute something you haven't experienced?"

Still other ghostly legends in PT concern beautiful Fort Worden State Park. One such tale is told about the Point Wilson lighthouse there. According to legend, Maria Hastings Littlefield, the wife of one of the lighthouse's keepers, still haunts the now-unoccupied keeper's house. She's looking for her only son, who drowned at the spot. Over the years, a woman in a long dress has been sighted around the place. Could it be Maria? Furthermore, there have been reports of a man seen in a downstairs kitchen and elsewhere around the house. There's speculation that he was a lighthouse keeper who lived there in the '20s and '30s and didn't want to leave.

Reports of ghostly presences have also been made about other parts of Fort Worden. In a 2009 article by Jennifer Jackson in the *Peninsula Daily News*, a night caretaker at the fort, Jeff Boyles, commented that he had never seen ghosts there. However, when he worked in the facility's old hospital building, he sometimes felt a strange presence: "When I first started working here, this is the one building that gave me the creeps. When I was at the bottom of the stairs, I'd get the feeling that someone was looking down the stairs at me. One time I heard a child crying."

And early one misty morning Boyles glimpsed an eerie moment from the fort's past, near what is now McCurdy Pavilion. He told Jackson, "I looked up and saw horses and wagons crossing the intersection. When I looked away and looked back, they were gone."

PORT ANGELES

Heading west along the northern shore of the Olympic Peninsula, travelers will come to Port Angeles, more of a working logging and fishing town than picturesque and tourist-oriented Port Townsend. As with Seattle's more famous underground, Port Angeles has an unusual "basement"—a warren of underground tunnels and rooms.

In 1914, a number of streets, walkways, and shops in Port Angeles's downtown were rebuilt, literally on top of existing buildings. The development takes in an area now bounded by Laurel Street on the east, Oak Street on the west, Front Street to the north, and First Street to the south.

This renovation was made in an effort to avoid some of the nasty side effects of living next to the Strait of Juan de Fuca. Whenever there was an especially high tide, water would flood the stores, hotels, and restaurants in the area. Not only was it destructive—it was stinky, too, considering the state of sewage treatment at the time.

The answer was to rebuild on pilings fourteen to sixteen feet above the existing streets. Although some of the existing buildings were raised on stilts, in other cases new buildings were simply erected on top of existing structures. That way, the new establishments had instant basements— but over time many of these underground chambers were abandoned, sealed up, or used to house utility lines. More recently, however, Port Angeles authorities approved a major renovation project that opened up the abandoned underground, creating in the process a new attraction for tourists—and a spooky one, at that.

It's proven to be so popular that a regular tour leads people through it, something that also happens in Seattle's underground. And, like so many allegedly haunted spots in the state, the Port Angeles underground has been investigated for paranormal activity. In 1999, the owner of the Port Angeles Underground Heritage Tour told *Peninsula Daily News* reporter Marcie Miller that a group of paranormal investigators photographed what they believed to be faces staring back through windows underground. The tour operator found the evidence unusual and, in the end, inconclusive. He told Miller, "I'm a skeptic, but that looks out of the ordinary."

Skeptic he may be, but plenty of other people aren't; they're convinced that there are indeed undead spirits down there. In fact, there has been speculation that they might be the ghosts of the many Chinese laborers who were brought over to the western United States during the early, rough-and-tumble days of settlement. The many "Chinatowns" that sprang up in the region's pioneer towns were closed, reclusive, and mysterious enclaves—and, people say, they may well harbor the spirits of their long-dead residents.

Chapter 8
Bellingham

Bellingham lies north of Seattle along Interstate 5, on the way to Vancouver, British Columbia. It's a college town—the home of Western Washington University—and the biggest urban area in mostly rural Whatcom County. But despite Bellingham's relatively small size, it's the home of a surprisingly large number of resident ghosts.

THE MOUNT BAKER THEATRE

Bellingham's most famous ghostly location is the Mount Baker Theatre, right downtown at 104 North Commercial Street. Opened in 1927, the beautifully ornate building features a Moorish-Spanish motif and an elaborate interior. It was a popular stop on the Pacific Northwest's vaudeville circuit and a regular venue for movie shows.

Spooky events have apparently been front and center at the Mount Baker from the start of the building's construction in 1927. In a 1996 article in the *Bellingham Herald*, Eldon Barrett and Ben Santarris wrote, "[T]he crews turned their first shovelfuls of soil to begin building the Moorish-Spanish structure, today one of Whatcom County's architectural treasures. But legend has it that the diggers disturbed more than just the soil, and lore about an unfettered stage specter has shadowed the Theatre ever since."

Since then, the Mount Baker has been the scene of dozens of reports about inexplicable phenomena, including strange noises and mysterious cold gusts of air. Ushers and other employees say they have witnessed other spooky doings, such as balls of light, ghostly footsteps, mysteriously closing doors, and sounds like the rustling of skirts—even after audiences have left the building.

The most commonly mentioned spirit in the theater is that of a woman. Theater employees have nicknamed her Judy (allegedly after Judy Garland, who once performed there). Some people speculate that Judy once owned the building and still wants to watch over her property.

But another version of the story concerns a young woman whose home was destroyed to make way for the building. She's said to haunt the corridor connecting the balcony and the mezzanine, and she seems especially interested in male employees, whose names she calls out. However, she appears to be harmless. In the *Herald* piece, Margaret Mackay, who was the house manager when she was interviewed, was quoted as saying, "Not to worry. I don't think she's malicious."

Reporters Barrett and Santarris also quoted Barry Bonifas, who was then the facility's executive director. Bonifas claimed to have a photo of the spirit, in the form of a hazy apparition near the building's balcony. He stated, "We are thinking maybe we got a picture of the ghost."

On the other hand, not everyone is convinced. Among the skeptics is Ruth Shaw, who was the Mount Baker's manager from 1984 to 1994. About those people who saw apparitions, Shaw notes, "Their theatrical imaginations, already fertile ground for ghost stories, were stirred by the sensations of a creaky, drafty, old building with rich imagery painted and sculptures in the theater's interior. Faces of angels, nymphs, dragons, griffins, gargoyles, people, and animals populate the walls of the theater. From the lobby, an imaginative person looking into the orchestra pit can make out the shape of a coffin."

So Judy may be hooey. On the other hand, maybe every old theater has—or should have, anyway—a resident ghost like her.

BAYVIEW CEMETERY

Bayview Cemetery, founded in the 1880s, is the final resting place for many of Whatcom County's most famous citizens, both early settlers and more current (but late) residents. The cemetery is a little east of downtown, not far from Whatcom Falls Park.

One of Bayview's supernatural attractions is the so-called Deathbed. The Deathbed is a flat gravestone that, according to legend, will hasten the death of anyone foolish enough to lie on it. (In other words, people say, it's an instrument of slow-motion suicide.)

According to historian Jeff Jewell of the Whatcom Museum of History & Art, the Deathbed is actually the resting place of Edmond L. Gaudette and his first wife, who died in 1910 of tuberculosis. A statue was put over her grave, and Gaudette was buried in the same plot after his death in 1916 of a stroke. His second wife, Laura, was slated to rest there as well, but her death in 1925 led to a family legal battle and an eventual burial in Seattle. The space reserved for her is still empty—but apparently the Deathbed next to it is not.

ANGEL EYES

Another of Bayview's spooky spots is a monument called Angel Eyes. This statue is located near the western edge of the cemetery, under a grove of oak and maple trees. According to one version of the story, on full moon nights the statue's eyes glow red. According to another tale, blood occasionally oozes from its eyes.

People have speculated that beneath the statue are the remains of a young woman killed because people suspected her of witchcraft. Skeptics, meanwhile, point out that, first of all, white settlers didn't arrive in the region until a couple hundred years after the witch trials in New England, and that in any case there has never been any evidence of witchcraft-related deaths in or near Bellingham.

Furthermore, according to the archives of the *Bellingham Herald,* the Angel Eyes grave, dating from 1910, is that of pioneer William H. Bland, along with his two wives and other family members. Apparently despondent over sickness in the family and a downturn in his financial affairs, Bland committed suicide in the basement of the Whatcom County Courthouse. Could this grisly and sad end to the pioneer's life have led to today's ghost stories?

THE LADY IN GREEN

Bayview Cemetery is by no means the only haunted spot in Bellingham. For example, there's a story connected to a place in the Fairhaven neighborhood: the hundred-plus-year-old Sycamore Building on the corner of 12th and Harris. Once a fashionable location for businesses and clubs, over the years it has played host to, among other notable figures, President William Taft and Mark Twain.

According to legend, things began when a young woman named Flora Blakely and her husband, John, moved into an apartment there in 1890. Flora died two years later, perhaps in childbirth, but her spirit didn't leave the building.

The Lady in Green, as she's now known, continues to haunt the building, which now largely has been given over to office space. Unexplained laughter and music have been heard there, and there's further evidence of ghostly happenings as well. A number of people who work there say that their office chairs face different ways when they arrive in the morning—specifically, they're pointed toward Bellingham Bay, as if someone had been there to watch the sunset.

And then there's the Old Town Café, which is housed in a historic building downtown at 316 West Holly Street. Nighttime employees have reported seeing dishes rise up into the air by themselves and return safely to their shelves minutes later. Others report hearing piano music, even though there's no piano in the restaurant or at any nearby locale. Furthermore, people walking past the building claim to have seen a woman looking down from the second-floor window when the place should have been unoccupied.

THE ELDRIDGE MANSION

A fourth allegedly haunted locale in Bellingham is the Eldridge Mansion at 2915 Eldridge Avenue, so named for the family that owned it (and, of course, that lent its name to the street). Built in 1926, the mansion is the third house erected on the site. (The first two burned to the ground.) It's an ornate and dramatic sight, built in a French Chateau-esque style. The imposing building *looks* like it ought to be haunted, even if the stories about it should prove to be just stories.

In any case, the mansion's current owners, Mike and Cis Kennard, say that there have been some unusual experiences there. Locked doors have been mysteriously found open (or vice-versa). A friend who was standing on a stool to adjust a blind in an upstairs room thought her husband had come into the room and had put a steadying hand on her shoulder—but he'd been downstairs all the time. Witnesses say they have also heard disembodied voices and bloodcurdling screams there. Since the mansion is now privately owned, you won't be able to check it out personally—but if you're lucky you might hear strange noises coming down Eldridge Avenue. . . .

Chapter 9
The San Juan
Islands

*The San Juan Islands in the far northwest corner of the state—
remote, isolated, beautiful, and often windy, foggy, and rainy—are,
in many ways, the perfect breeding grounds for ghostly stories. Not
only that; some of the islands' residents, according to legend, are
reluctant to give up their lives of splendid isolation even if they've
gone on to ghosthood. Reporter Heather Larson, writing in the Spokane* Spokesman-Review *in 2007, commented, "People settle in
the San Juan Islands off the Western Washington coast for a variety of reasons. Some like the slow pace, others fancy farming. Some
enjoy the serenity and natural beauty, and still others simply hang
around—even after they have passed."*

SAN JUAN ISLAND

Blakely Island—population much less than one hundred and
with no public ferry—is the location for one of the region's
most famous, enduring, and perplexing ghost stories. In 1895,
a schoolteacher named Richard Straub killed a man named
Leon Lanterman. According to Straub's version of the incident, he was keeping Lanterman from attacking a teenager,
Irving Parberry. (Another version is that the reason for the
killing was a land dispute between Straub and Lanterman.)

After the murder, Straub and Parberry rowed to San Juan
Island, the largest and most populated of the island group,

so that Straub could confess to authorities. He apparently believed that it was justifiable homicide and that he would be exonerated. Quoted in a 2011 article by reporter Cali Bagby of the *Journal of the San Juans,* local historian Robin Jacobson commented, "It's a really sad story. He probably didn't think he would be hanged."

But he was wrong. Straub spent the next two years in either the San Juan Island jail or its counterpart in Bellingham, on the mainland. In time, Straub was tried in a courtroom set up in Friday Harbor's Odd Fellows Hall. The large venue was chosen over the county courthouse so that the public could buy tickets and attend the exciting event.

Straub was convicted in 1895, later that same year. In the only execution ever carried out on San Juan Island, he was hanged. According to legend, Straub's body was never claimed, and its whereabouts today are unknown. He may lie buried at Point Caution, just north of Friday Harbor, at what was then a military reservation.

Today, a number of people claim to have felt a ghostly presence at what is now the Whale Museum, the building in which Straub was tried. One of these people was a supervisor who was overlooking the building's renovation when it was converted to house the museum. While the work was going on, she frequently slept upstairs in a loft area. One night she woke up to see a tall, dark-haired man standing in the doorway—a description that would fit Straub to a T.

On the other hand, Jacobson, the island historian, told reporter Bagby that the spirit the supervisor saw may in fact be that of someone else—Sheriff Newton Jones, the lawman who presided over the notorious Straub case. Jones's descendants say that the trial and execution affected the sheriff greatly. Soon after the trial, the sheriff's wife died, he moved off the island, and he himself died later after years of a troubled, sad exile—in Bagby's words, he was "never to return—at least not in human form."

ADAH BEENY

Also on San Juan Island, people tell the story of Adah Beeny (identified in some sources as Ada Beane). Adah (let's call her that) came to Roche Harbor at the northern tip of the island as a twenty-year-old in the early 1900s. She held a variety of jobs over the next few years, primarily as a nanny for the five children of John McMillin, a prominent Tacoma businessman who had a home on the island. McMillin's wealth, in large part, came from mining operations to extract the rich limestone deposits on the island. (His mine is now the site of the plush Roche Harbor Resort.)

Besides nannying, Adah also worked for a time as McMillin's secretary/bookkeeper. She was close to the McMillin family and lived in a small cottage next to the family home. In fact, she was so close to them that after her death her ashes were kept for a time in one of the McMillin sons' offices. These remains were later transferred to the Afterglow Mausoleum, the family's elaborate resting place north near Roche Harbor.

That mausoleum, by the way, is pretty spooky by itself— well worth the half-mile hike to reach it, passing through a forest and a small old cemetery. It's not, shall we say, your standard resting place. Based on classical Roman architecture, the Afterglow's main feature is a circle of limestone pillars that ring a table and seven chairs, also made of limestone. The whole thing is set on a raised dais made of—what else?—limestone. There are winding stairs leading from the ground up to the dais; the pillars, according to the apparently philosophical McMillin, represent the winding path of life. Furthermore, one of the pillars was deliberately left broken, a touch that reflects what McMillin called the "unfinished state of man's work when the string of life is broken."

This unusual monument to a deep-thinking business-man and his family, not surprisingly, has been the source of a ghostly legend or two. Notably, there have been reports over the years that visitors have spotted the McMillin family sitting around the table atop their mausoleum, laughing and talking.

But back to Adah. It's believed by some of the island's residents that her presence is, on occasion, felt inside the restaurant of the charming Hotel de Haro. McMillin built this imposing establishment in 1886, and over the years it has hosted such dignitaries as President Theodore Roosevelt.

Specifically, our Adah is thought to be responsible for such events as the spontaneous shattering of several glass shelves in the hotel's gift shop and a storm door that opens on its own. But she's generally a benign presence and sensing her, so they say, is just a fleeting awareness of slight unease; Jacobson, the local historian, comments, "Usually people just get a feeling that she's there, or see a shadow or hear a sound. It's usually a neutral or frightening feeling in the sense that it's not normal to feel a ghost, not that the ghost does anything frightening."

Meanwhile, the road leading into Roche Harbor is the scene of another mysterious phenomenon. It's said that along the road you can sometimes spot the ghost of a bride murdered long ago, still dressed in an old-fashioned wedding dress.

And then there's False Bay on the island's southwest corner. The otherworldly legend about False Bay concerns what the locals call the Cry Baby House. This was a private house that allegedly burned down in the 1990s, leaving only a vacant, desolate field—and, reportedly, the occasional sound of a crying baby who met a grisly end when the building went up in flames.

ORCAS ISLAND

Out on another of the San Juans—beautiful Orcas Island— it's believed that another spirit is in residence. This is the ghost of Alice Rheem, who lived there between the world wars. In the 1930s, Alice's husband bought the property that today is luxurious Rosario Resort. His name was Donald Rheem, and he was a well-off industrialist and inventor from California.

Details are skimpy, but it appears that Alice was a girl who liked to have fun and liked her liquor a little too much. In any case, soon into their marriage Rheem stayed in California but sent Alice to live on his property in what surely seemed like deep exile.

Not surprisingly, Alice caused quite a stir when she arrived on the rustic island with her risqué, big-city ways. Among other pastimes, she liked to ride a Harley motorcycle around the island and play cards with local men down at the general store—behavior that was most shocking and quite the opposite of the conservative ways of most Orcas residents.

Alice stayed on the island for most of her life and died of alcohol-related causes in 1956. But it's said her presence lingers on, and it can still be seen on occasion around Orcas. The old girl is apparently as saucy as ever, since she's often spotted wearing nothing more than a red negligee. She's also presumably responsible for the suggestive sounds that can sometimes be heard coming from unoccupied rooms at the resort—the sounds of moans and squeaking bedsprings.

Elsewhere on the island, the one-hundred-plus-year-old landmark Orcas Hotel overlooking the island's ferry dock is the source of the legend of Octavia Van Moorhem, whose family bought the hotel in 1905. It's had quite a history, especially in the days when liquor was illegal, as a report prepared in 1974 for the National Register of Historic Places notes:

> Octavia Van Moorhem ran the hotel as a summer resort for 36 years, while her husband Constant ran the store. The original site included a large area with kitchen, gardens and a small farm. They added the present dining room in 1916. . . .
>
> During prohibition there was a bank robbery in Canada, and a bullet hole in the front porch post of the hotel reminds islanders of how robbers fought it out with the Sheriff on the steps of the hotel.

As with high-spirited Alice Rheem, it's said that Octavia is still with us. She can allegedly be heard pacing up and down the floors of her hotel. A 2002 piece by Diane Mapes in the *Seattle Times* quotes the current owner as saying that guests have often heard strange noises, such as footsteps overhead in areas where there are no real floors to walk on—just ceiling joists.

Octavia is also apparently responsible for other unexplained phenomena in the hotel, such as lights and water faucets that turn on and off by themselves. People have also reported other inexplicable occurrences, including strange sounds coming from the walls and weird reflections that appear behind them in mirrors.

Nonetheless, the spirit that causes these phenomena is apparently harmless. The manager commented about Octavia, "[S]he's friendly. Although she really put a scare into some workmen who were renovating the place back in '85. Octavia appeared out of nowhere, hissing and screaming. Poor guys ran all the way down to the tavern."

Part Three

SOUTHWEST, CENTRAL, AND EASTERN WASHINGTON

Chapter 10

Southwest
Washington

Southwest Washington roughly includes the small counties of Grays Harbor, Pacific, Wahkiakum, Lewis, Cowlitz, Clark, and Skamania. One of the region's claims to fame is that it includes the mouth of the mighty, mighty Columbia River—the end point of the famous Lewis and Clark Trail. (Hence, two of the region's counties bear the names of the explorers.) Elsewhere, Southwest Washington boasts miles of rugged coastline, wide and gentle beaches, and ample land for logging and water for fishing. The towns that grew up to service those industries have fallen on hard times as their livelihoods have shrunk, but the area's still fascinating—and, of course, full of ghostly legends, too.

ABERDEEN: THE SPIRIT OF BILLY GOHL

Aberdeen, in Grays Harbor County on the central-southwest coast of the state, plays a seminal role in rock music history. The blue-collar town, once a thriving port, is now known to the outside world as the birthplace of Kurt Cobain and the boyhood home of Krist Novoselic. The musicians, two-thirds of the band Nirvana, grew up in the town and first made music together there.

But Aberdeen has at least one other claim to fame: It was the home of a notorious killer whose spirit, it's said, lingers on in the building where he used to work.

Today, Billy Gohl's memory is kept alive by a watering hole named in his honor. Billy's Bar and Grill is housed in a brick building just blocks from the Chehalis River. An early tenant was a fraternal organization called the Sailor's Union of the Pacific. During the late nineteenth and early twentieth centuries, when Aberdeen was a wide-open, rough-and-tumble town, the sailors who put into port routinely stopped by. There they could collect their mail, find old friends, and safely leave valuables (well, more or less safely).

Sailors in port are, well, sailors in port, and the ones who hove to in Aberdeen were no different. They were looking to spend their money, and there were plenty of gamblers, saloonkeepers, and women who were eager to help them. So a man could get a drink and a meal on the ground floor of the Sailor's Union, and on the second floor he could get certain other needs met.

A major turning point in the history of the Sailor's Union came in 1903. This was when Wilhelm F. "Billy" Gohl was hired on as a bartender. Not much about Billy's early life is known; although he claimed at different times to be from Germany or Austria, police reports credited Madison, Wisconsin, or Bergen, Norway, as his birthplace.

It's said that Billy had a baby face and candid blue eyes, but he was a good-sized fellow, and apparently this was put to good use in ending barroom fights. His strength was used in other ways as well. When he met a seafarer who had money but no relatives, he'd get the hapless sailor drunk, knock him out, take his money, and, as often as not, kill him. According to one version of the story, Billy sent his victims careening down a chute from the building directly into the Wishkah River. Another version has him using a small launch to take the bodies far out into the harbor before dumping them. So many sailors went missing over the years that Aberdeen became known as the Port of Missing Men.

Dozens of crimes have also been attributed to Billy. After he took on a job as a Sailor's Union official in addition to bartending, he committed some of these crimes in his official capacity, typically breaking up strikes illegally or threatening non-union sailors. Another example of Billy's antisocial behavior: Once, he abducted a group of non-union crewmen from the schooner *Fearless* and threatened them unless they moved on.

But he also carried on a thriving side business as a free-lance crook. According to legend, Billy loved to talk about his deeds. Any chat with him would quickly turn into a monologue about how he'd burgled this house or killed that man or set fire to some rival's business. Maybe he'd tell you about stealing a boat or shooting a deer out of season. One of Billy's favorite stories about himself had him eating another man while trapped by a blizzard in the Yukon.

Billy got away with his crimes for some time, and he got others to help. The late historian Murray Morgan, in an article for the Tacoma Historical Society, had this to say about him: "Billy could be remarkably persuasive. A man who shot a friend at Gohl's suggestion told a jury, 'Billy looked at me and said, "You take him," and I knew I had to. There wasn't anything else to do. He had a great deal of animal magnetism.'"

One of Billy's worst crimes came after he got into an argument with the bar's owner and was fired. To get his revenge, Billy burned the place to the ground. Two men died, including the owner.

It's believed that Billy was responsible for some forty murders, with other estimates ranging much higher, but in the end he was convicted of only two. In 1910, Billy was sentenced to life in the penitentiary. He later was moved to a mental institution and died there in 1928.

But it's said that "Billy Ghoul" never really left Aberdeen. Specifically, rumor has it that his spirit still makes itself known in the bar where he used to work. There are frequent reports of unexplainable cold spots around the place, especially in summer. Lights flicker for no apparent reason, and doors open and close mysteriously. According to some sources, shot glasses and mugs behind or on the bar periodically fly across the room and smash into the wall. Similar events have been reported in the kitchen, where objects have been known to fly off shelves and hit the walls and floor.

Furthermore, the ghosts of several prostitutes have been reported hanging around upstairs. And a silent, staring man is said to have appeared one night, bellying up to the bar. When an employee approached him, the man vanished. Could this and other eerie incidents at Billy's Bar and Grill be examples of the hotheaded murderer's spirit losing his temper?

WILLAPA BAY

If you head south of Aberdeen and hug the coast, you'll come to Willapa Bay. Along its northern shore is the tiny fishing town of Tokeland. (No, the town's name doesn't come from what you're thinking. It's in honor of a nineteenth-century Native American chief.)

One of the town's establishments, the Tokeland Hotel, has been a popular vacation destination since its origins as the Kindred Inn in the late nineteenth century. It's also one of the most thoroughly investigated locations in the state for paranormal explorers.

In the case of the Tokeland Hotel, the spirit is named Charley. The story goes that, in life, Charley was an illegal immigrant who had been smuggled into the country from China in the 1930s. He allegedly died while at the hotel. (It's unclear what a presumably poor illegal immigrant was doing staying at a popular resort destination. It's a reasonable assumption that he was working there.)

In any case, it's alleged that Charley still occupies the top floor of the vintage building and can occasionally be seen roaming around the halls. There have also been incidents such as diners' plates in the hotel's restaurant jumping up and spinning around. And another story is that a ghostly cat can be seen in the hotel, although no cat lives there. Furthermore, according to some reports, Room Seven is the single most haunted spot in the place. According to this legend, Room Seven was the site, long ago, of a grisly murder.

Farther south on Willapa Bay, you'll come to the town of Raymond. Raymond is the home of the Hannan Playhouse, which originated in 1913 as the town's Polish Hall. The building fell into disrepair over the years, but in 1969 it was remodeled as a venue for a local theater group, the Willapa Players.

During the remodeling process, people started reporting strange doings: footsteps coming from the attic, doors opening and closing mysteriously, props moving by themselves from one side of the stage to the other, and a cat who suddenly appeared onstage, walked its length, and just as suddenly disappeared where there was no exit. Furthermore, a worker once noticed footprints in dust on the stage at a time when no person could have been there.

Then there's the story of a Polish immigrant named Oscar. Oscar died in the building back when it was the

Polish Hall, but he is still sometimes spotted there, hanging around to see the shows now that it's a playhouse. According to legend, this ghost is a shy fellow. He never makes himself known during a performance—only when the actors are rehearsing or preparing for a performance.

There are occasional reports of other ghostly events in the theater, including voices that can be heard coming from far-off, unoccupied corners of the building. Actors rehearsing their roles sometimes also hear laughter inexplicably coming from seats at the back of the hall. This laughter is generally well received; on the theater group's website, one of the Willapa Players comments, "If we're rehearsing a comedy, the chuckles are as good as a standing ovation (if the scene is a serious drama, we know we need to work harder)."

Furthermore, it's said that the Hannan Playhouse is on occasion the location for other signs of ghostly presences. Among these: a spot in the lobby that is so cold it makes one's skin feel like ice, while the rest of the lobby is toasty warm.

ILWACO AND THE LONG BEACH PENINSULA

Farther south, near the mouth of the mighty Columbia River, we find three connected locations with reports of paranormal activity: the fishing town of Ilwaco, the resort destination of Long Beach, and the slender Long Beach Peninsula.

Perhaps the best-known ghost tale from the region involves the North Head lighthouse, on the north side of the Columbia's mouth and just outside Ilwaco. This story relates the sad death of Mary Pesonen in 1923.

North Head is a rugged, rainy, and windswept part of the world (where wind speeds of over one hundred miles per hour are not unusual). It's also the scene of many shipwrecks, so back in those days the lighthouse—nearly two hundred feet up a sheer cliff from the crashing surf—played a vital role in keeping shipping lanes as safe as possible.

As the story goes, the first keeper at North Head was Finnish-born Alexander K. Pesonen. A few years after beginning his work there, Pesonen married an Irishwoman named Mary Watson. The couple lived in the small house adjoining the lighthouse. For nearly a quarter-century, Mary was kept busy cleaning and cooking for her husband and his assistants, who lived nearby.

But Mary was apparently prone to depression, and the gloomy environment and isolation of the lighthouse could not have helped. Doctors in Portland, Oregon, to the east and on the other side of the river, diagnosed her with what was then called melancholia and treated her as best they could. But her mental illness proved to be intractable.

Soon after her return to the lighthouse from Portland, she grew despondent again, and early in the morning of June 8, 1923, threw herself over the cliff while walking her dog. A headline in the *Seattle Daily Times* of June 10, 1923, read, "Wife of Lighthouse Keeper Commits Suicide by Plunge Down Rocks—Dog Guides Master to Fateful Spot."

The newspaper article went on to explain: "In ill health for weeks, the woman went for a walk, accompanied by her dog. Soon the animal returned to the lighthouse, whining. Mr. Pesonen followed the dog, which led him to the spot where his wife had leaped. Her coat was on the ground and it was easy to see the course down the rocky cliff which her body had taken, until it struck the water."

Frank Hammond, one of Pesonen's assistants, bravely risked his life to recover the body from the bottom of the cliff, and Mary Pesonen today rests in Ilwaco Cemetery.

In September of the same year, Pesonen retired, but in 1925 he suffered a fatal heart attack and was buried next to his wife.

In the years since, there have been many reports of Mary's spirit making appearances at the lighthouse, looking appropriately melancholy. Apparently, however, her late husband has not made a similar appearance.

Farther north up the Long Beach Peninsula, legend has it that a number of local places are haunted. One report asserts that the spirit of a child who died in the historic town of Oysterville, at the far tip of the peninsula, can sometimes be sensed at the vintage schoolhouse there. Another town on the peninsula, Seaview, also has a spot supposedly inhabited by spirits: Rod's Lamplighter Restaurant, where patrons have reported sensing a ghostly presence who likes to play pool and play tricks, such as turning lights on and off.

According to this legend, the apparition is the spirit of the Lamplighter's former owner, a man named Louie Sloan. In 1992, the *Seattle Times* reported that after Sloan's death his cremated ashes lay abandoned for years in a local chapel. However, they have since been brought back to the Lamplighter and now rest on a mantle there—and sometimes show up as a pool-playing spirit.

FORT VANCOUVER

Vancouver (not to be confused with the city of the same name in British Columbia) is directly across the Columbia River from Portland, Oregon. It's much smaller than neighboring Portland, but it has its own good-sized share of ghost stories. Most of them are connected to Fort Vancouver, which is today a national historic site. (Over the years, the military facility has also been known as Vancouver Barracks.)

Originally, the fort's primary purpose was to protect the interests of Great Britain's commercial operation there, the Hudson's Bay Company. Hudson's Bay had exclusive trading rights there, primarily for furs, and needed to maintain security. Built in 1824, the fort was named for the British explorer Captain George Vancouver, who did much to explore and map the Pacific Northwest. It was also a destination, or at least a stopping point, for settlers traveling the Oregon Trail in search of land. As a result, a variety of ethnicities passed through, and the languages spoken included Canadian French, Spanish, Chinook Jargon, and even Hawaiian.

As England's fur trade began to dwindle, the United States gradually assumed control of the region. In 1849 the US Army set up barracks nearby and by 1860 Hudson's Bay closed down its operations, ensuring American control of the region and of Fort Vancouver itself.

Six years later, much of the original fort burned down and was rebuilt. Fort Vancouver was designated as a national monument in 1948, and it became a national historic site in 1961. In 2011, it closed as an active military post.

With all that history, and with so many people passing through it for all those years, it's not surprising that Fort Vancouver has its share of ghosts. A group of local history buffs, the Vancouver Heritage Ambassadors, gives tours of the fort that emphasize these spooky aspects of its story. Quoted by reporter Mike Bailey of the *Clark County Columbian* in 2007, Bobbi Fox, president of the organization, commented, "This [tour] is a spiced-up version of history. We've added a gossipy feel to the stories that are mildly spooky. They aren't exactly G-rated, but they are appropriate for all members of the family."

One of these stories is a persistent rumor that the ghostly image of an American Indian woman periodically appears, frightening passersby out of their wits. She shows up near the intersection of Evergreen Boulevard and Fort Vancouver Way along Officers Row (which is now primarily a street of beautiful restored houses). Reports made by residents and former residents, as well as by a number of newspaper clippings over the years, have bolstered this legend.

Also on Officers Row is the restored building known as the Ulysses S. Grant House. Before his stints as a Civil War general and US president, Grant was the fort's quartermaster. (Actually, Grant never lived in the 1849 house, but what's in a name?) Today the building is a popular restaurant, and legend has it that a presence nicknamed Sully haunts its kitchen to make mischief.

There are plenty of other eerie legends about Fort Vancouver. One of these stems from an incident in 1982. Workers digging to find a water pipe in the basement of one of the fort's buildings discovered that it was built directly over a cemetery that dated from the mid-1800s. Archaeologists uncovered the remnants of coffins and the bones of nineteenth-century members of the Cowlitz tribe of Native Americans, which had been left behind when remains from the cemetery's marked graves were moved elsewhere.

In 1993 Lieutenant Colonel Ward Jones, commanding officer of the post, asked Roy Wilson, a Cowlitz holy man, to perform a cleansing ceremony for the spirits of these dead souls. Wilson used smoke from burning sage and an eagle feather to free the spirits from the remnants of their earthly lives. Wilson told a reporter for the Associated Press, "The old tradition is that spirits would stay in a disturbed area unless released from the earth. We don't think of it as haunting, but they were present here before the ceremony. We believe that after what happened today they will be happy." The remains were then reburied at the site.

Wilson's prayers may have eased the final sleep of the deceased, but Jones and other barracks personnel continue to report unexplained spirits. Jones told *Columbian* reporter Brett Oppegaard in 1995, "If you work late at night, you can hear footsteps upstairs, people talking and doors opening and closing. I just figure it's a co-existence. We work during the day, and they work during the night. . . . They're just here doing their job while we do ours."

Oppegaard also spoke with Richard Reed, a civilian barracks employee who works in one of the buildings where several sightings have been reported. Reed commented, "I used to come to work about 5 a.m., and one morning I was in my office when I heard footsteps upstairs. Nobody was supposed to be there so I went upstairs. I could hear footsteps going down the hallway, about six feet in front of me. But nobody was there. I followed them down the stairs. When they got to the door, it swung open by itself and then shut. It kind of upset me, but after listening to the same thing for months, I got used to it."

Furthermore, a sergeant staying in the same building for two weeks said that he was awakened twice by a loud command of "ten-hut" and the clicking of boots together. Later he woke up again at the sound of someone playing pool. He ran upstairs to the room where the pool table was located; no one was in the room, but the pool balls were still moving.

Meanwhile, across the river in Oregon City—but still officially part of the Fort Vancouver National Site—is a house, built in the 1840s, that served as the retirement home of Dr. John McLoughlin and his family. During his long career as a public servant, McLoughlin helped establish Fort Vancouver and served as the chief factor—essentially the region's governor—in what was then called the Oregon Country.

The good doctor died in 1846, and it's said that his ghost still haunts his house, making itself known by heavy footsteps heard up and down the halls. There have also been reports of mysterious people appearing in the windows of the house's lookout tower. Another version of the story has McLoughlin's spirit wandering around Fort Vancouver itself.

OTHER VANCOUVER HAUNTINGS

Fort Vancouver is not the only place in the area with a legend of hauntings. Another ghostly story revolves around a mysterious death that occurred in the town of Vancouver in 1920. An article from that year in the (Vancouver) *Evening Columbian* reported the event that kicked off the sad tale:

PERCIVAL IS BELIEVED TO HAVE PASSED KALAMA, WA.
RALPH PERCIVAL UNABLE TO FIND FURTHER
TRACE OF FATHER, HOWEVER.

R.G. Percival, son of Mayor G.R. Percival, of Vancouver, who has been missing for several weeks, was in Kalama [north of Vancouver] this week investigating clues that have led him to believe that his father passed this way and went on farther.

A barber here was almost certain that he shaved the missing man Tuesday following his disappearance.

Young Percival in conversation here said that his father apparently did not strip himself of all means of identification and that prior to his departure he did nothing unusual.

The son is visiting all the farmhouses along the road hoping to find a place where his father may have stopped . . . While a stranger answering the general description of the mayor was in Kalama on the day mentioned, Percival declared, he was unable to find further trace of him.

Some ten days later, Mayor Percival's body was found, hanging in a grove of trees on the Oregon side of the Columbia, roughly one hundred yards from today's Interstate Bridge. Other accounts place the tragic scene on Hayden Island, in the Columbia River between Vancouver and Portland.

No matter where the body was found, it apparently is still active in the form of an otherworldly apparition: the Interstate Bridge Ghost. There have been several reported sightings of the spirit of Mayor Percival. According to these reports, he is well dressed in a dark hat and overcoat, walking slowly across the bridge as if he was tracing the route to his death.

There are plenty of other spooky stories to be heard in Vancouver. One of the best known of these centers on a vintage brick home on West 13th Street, which today is a Greek restaurant called the Touch of Athens Hidden House. In this version of the familiar haunted-restaurant theme, the resident spirit is fond of singing and playing pranks. Employees have also reported bathrooms that lock from the inside, inexplicably mixed up or falling utensils, and voices heard while the place is being cleaned up at night.

MOUNT ST. HELENS, CHEHALIS, AND CENTRALIA

Mount St. Helens, northeast of Vancouver in the Gifford Pinchot National Forest, is a familiar name to millions because of its spectacular eruption in the spring of 1980. But the region around St. Helens has another claim to fame: reports of a ghostly female hitchhiker.

Legend has it that a woman in white has been encountered, hitching rides up and down the roads around St. Helens. When a driver stops, so they say, she gets in the backseat and, in the course of conversation, predicts that the mountain will erupt within a specific two-day period—and disappears while the car is in motion. (She's apparently not completely informed.)

According to an article in the *Seattle Post-Intelligencer*, the police chief of nearby Morton commented on one occasion, "We picked up a rumor that some people picked up a lady with a white gown on. She gave her warning and when they looked in the back seat she was gone. And they were going sixty miles an hour down the road. But I don't know what they were smokin' or drinkin'."

Meanwhile, over in the town of Chehalis, *Lewis County Chronicle* reporters Eric Schwartz and Dan Schreiber set a ghostly scene in an article from 2008: "The sounds of children on century-old steps. Creaks and noises above a historic train depot. Unexplained 'guests' in a downtown hotel and watering hole. It seems that no matter where someone goes in Lewis County, tales of hauntings and ghosts will follow. From the long and storied history of the area, dozens of ghost stories have emerged."

One notable legend stems from a ghastly murder committed early in the twentieth century. According to an anonymously written article of 1912 in the *Chehalis Chronicle*, the victim's body was found near what then was the Northern Pacific Railway Depot, and is now the home of the Lewis County Historical Museum.

His identity remained a mystery for several months before he was identified as a man named Layman. Unsubstantiated legend has it that the victim had been beaten and his legs cut off. The story goes on to say that his spirit remains there, sitting on a staircase. (In another version, he appears in the historical society's research library.)

In Schwartz and Schreiber's article, Debbie Knapp, then the museum's director, commented that she wasn't sure if ghosts really haunted her place of employment. However, Knapp told the reporters that she did have one "creepy" experience: "I was here late, by myself, and I heard someone sneeze. I decided that it was probably a good time to leave for the night."

Meanwhile, Jill Kangas, an emergency planner for the Lewis County Sheriff's Office, saw and heard more than just a sneeze. Kangas was one of the leaders of the volunteer group that restored the depot to its present status as a museum. According to her, strange things happened during the renovation process: "You'd hear drawers open. You'd hear the old-fashioned roller chairs rolling across the ground. Very often, we'd hear roll-top desks closing, and that's a very unique sound . . . but there weren't any there."

Late one night—alone—Kangas had an even closer encounter with the unexplainable. Per her usual routine, she locked the entrances when she was there but no one else was around. When it was time to go home, Kangas walked into the narrow closet where the breaker switches are for the building's lights. "I got down to the sixth row of breakers, and I heard this voice behind me," Kangas said. "I heard this voice say, 'Excuse me, ma'am.'"

In the doorway, Kangas said she saw a petite young woman, slight and perhaps in her late teens, dressed in a

late 1890s-style black wool dress and holding a small crocheted travel bag in her folded hands. Kangas told the newspaper, "She probably weighed about 85 pounds . . . had her
hair coming up in curls on the side with a black bonnet tied
on the side with a big sash. She turned around and looked
at me and said, 'Has the train come yet?' She turned around
and took one step in the hallway, turned to the right, took
three steps on the terrazzo (floor), and nothing."

Panicked, Kangas slammed the door, ran from the
museum, and locked herself in her car.

Another time, Kangas says, she and two tourists saw a
slender conductor in what once was the train conductor's
office at the far end of the depot. He was walking back and
forth, writing notes on a clipboard—but he wasn't flesh
and blood.

Kangas says that what she has witnessed still disturbs
her: "It makes the hair come up on the back of my neck just
to think about it. . . . I don't think I have clairvoyance or
ESP. I'm just an average person secure enough to tell about
what I saw. If it gives someone else peace about what they
might have seen, that's good."

Just north of Chehalis is Centralia, which holds a place
of honor in Washington State labor history as the site of a
bloody battle in 1919 between anti-unionizing members of
the American Legion and the pro-union Industrial Workers
of the World (better known as Wobblies). The Centralia Massacre, as it's known, left six people dead and several more
wounded, and it led to many prison sentences. Although
there are no recorded tales of ghostly remnants of this
bloody bit of history, it is not hard to imagine that the
passion of the cause and the deadly battle between the two
factions has resulted in the continuing presence of spirits.

One enduring spooky story about Centralia is that of the 1908-vintage Olympic Club Hotel and Theater on Tower Avenue, now part of the McMenamins chain. A 2010 article by Nikki Talotta in a Tacoma newspaper, the *Weekly Volcano*, calls this place "perhaps the best-known haunted building in the Pacific Northwest." While that may be hyperbole, stories nonetheless regularly surface about strange goings-on there.

The cause of these disturbances, so the story goes, is the spirit of one Louis Galba, who was injured in a fire shortly after the place opened and died several months later as a result of his injuries. What goes on, so it's said, is the usual: strange and inexplicable voices, mysterious knockings, fire alarms tripping for no reason, cold feelings, doors that open and close by themselves, and candles that spontaneously light and snuff themselves out.

Emily Owen, a server, told reporters Schwartz and Schreiber (who also wrote about the place) that unexplained events occur with some regularity in the Olympic Club's upper mezzanine, formerly a card room, and in its basement, once a Prohibition-era speakeasy. She's heard many stories over the years, including ones about chairs inexplicably rearranging themselves in a pyramid in the basement and an axe that mysteriously fell from above and nearly struck an employee.

But Owen has also had her own run-ins with the supernatural. While closing down the club one night, she made a point to put out all of the table candles on the mezzanine, only to find something strange was happening: "I came up here and put them all out and nobody else was here except the other closer. I happened to walk down and look back here and all the candles were lit again. . . . Nobody had gone up here."

The *Chronicle* article also quotes Sara McFarland, another Olympic Club server, who says that she and other employees usually keep the jukebox playing while closing down the restaurant. On occasion, however, the normal music was drowned out by a mysterious tune. She commented, "All of the [*sic*] sudden over the top of the jukebox music this old, weird ragtime piano music comes on. We don't know where it comes from. . . . That's happened to us twice."

And let's not forget the haunted steps off Lincoln Creek Road west of Centralia. This flight of concrete steps begins to rise from the road and continues into a lightly wooded area. According to legend, the steps once led to a schoolhouse that was destroyed when it burned to the ground—with children inside. If visitors go there at the right time, so it's said, they can hear the voices of children and feel a cold, disturbing presence.

Meanwhile, down in tiny Cathlamet, across the Columbia River from Westport, Oregon, is Hotel Cathlamet and the adjoining Pierre's Restaurant. According to Kari Kandoll, the curator of the Wahkiakum County Historical Society, there's a legend about the hotel that a woman haunts the place. Although Kandoll says she has not felt the spirit's presence the last few times she's been there, there's always the possibility the woman will show up again. You just never know. . . .

Chapter 11

Central Washington and the Cascade Mountains

Roughly speaking, Central Washington is the western half of Eastern Washington. Got that? The confusion arises because most locals think of only two regions: Western Washington is west of the Cascade Mountains, and Eastern Washington is . . . well, you get the idea.

It may be easy to think of the Cascade Mountains as Central Washington's western border and its eastern border as an imaginary line that roughly corresponds with the eastern borders of Okanogan, Grant, and Benton Counties. Altogether, Central Washington takes in these counties as well as Chelan, Kittitas, Douglas, Yakima, and Klickitat Counties.

The region is one of the nation's great breadbaskets; it's the reason why Washington State is second from the top in the number of agricultural crops produced (more than 250—only California has more). The range of agriculture here is astonishing; for example, it produces some eleven billion (yes, billion) apples a year, more than half the nation's supply. The region is also among America's top wheat-growing regions. In 2010, it helped the state rank fourth in that regard (only North Dakota, Kansas, and Montana produced more). Grapes, raspberries, cherries, pears, mint, corn, potatoes—not to mention some great wine—all are abundant in this fertile region.

Beyond agriculture, Central Washington is home to plenty of other incredible stuff, including one of the great engineering feats of modern times—Grand Coulee Dam—and some amazing natural wonders, perhaps the best known being the powerful Columbia River, which snakes south through the region on its way to the Pacific. And speaking of incredible stuff—check out the abundant collection of ghost stories there.

YAKIMA

Yakima, in the heart of the fertile Yakima Valley, is Central Washington's largest city. As well as being the region's commercial and cultural hub, Yakima has another claim to fame: an unusually large assortment of ghosts and spirits.

According to legend, six to seven ghosts may haunt just one place—the Depot Restaurant and Lounge on North Front Street, housed in one of the many vintage buildings that grace the region.

The building, with its distinctive white tile dome, dates from 1910. It wasn't always a restaurant. The structure began life as a stop on the Northern Pacific Railway as the trainline snaked through the Yakima Valley. But a resting place for weary travelers was not its only function: It also served as an eerie and grim locale for the town's authorities to send bodies of the deceased on the next stages of their journeys.

During several deadly typhoid epidemics early in the twentieth century, Yakima residents had to use the station's furnace to cremate the many quickly decomposing bodies of disease victims.

Given the Depot's sad history, a tantalizing possibility remains. Could some of its victims be causing the spooky incidents reported in the building today?

The trains stopped running through Yakima in the early 1970s, and the old depot fell into disrepair for years. It found new life in 2002 when Karl Pasten and his wife Kristie leased part of the space and remodeled it as a railway-themed restaurant and bar.

Complete with ghosts.

All kinds of unusual things have been seen and heard in and around the Depot. Among them are the sounds of children playing and lively organ music coming from the attic—where, not surprisingly, there is no organ. Other unexplained events include faucets inexplicably turning off and doors shutting by themselves, plus a variety of strange noises and cold spots.

Most notable, however, are appearances by a ghostly woman dressed in a long white apron with her hair tied back in a bun. The toddler daughter of a Depot bartender, according to legend, once saw her and said she was pretty. The lady has been spotted, among other places, on a staircase leading to the building's attic.

Pasten used to scoff at the idea that his place was haunted. But he's heard so many stories from patrons and employees, and he's had so much attention from local ghost hunters, that he's less skeptical than before. True or not, he acknowledges, the stories are good for business. As Pasten told a reporter for the *Yakima Herald-Republic,* "The only thing I don't like about it is that the ghosts don't pay rent."

Just down the block from the Depot, you can find two other establishments that have reputations for being haunted. Both are in vintage buildings that have housed eating and drinking establishments for decades. Back in the early days, when Yakima was a wide-open town, they were part of a very lively neighborhood. The variety of diversions available there included drink, food, sleeping accommodations, gambling—and, of course, the company of friendly women.

The two haunted restaurants today are the Greystone (in the Lund Building) and Café Melange (in the Commercial Building).

Both joints, apparently, are catnip for ghosts. Quoted in a *Herald-Republic* article, Café Melange's owner, John Kilbourne, stated, "Just about anyone who has ever worked at either place has a ghost story to tell."

This isn't surprising, considering the checkered past histories of the restaurants. Both were once saloons well known for their upstairs brothels and occasional violence. Furthermore, the restaurants are in side-by-side buildings that have underground tunnels connecting them to other downtown buildings. Rumor has it these tunnels were used to hide white slaves early in the twentieth century—and were almost certainly used as hidey-holes for booze during Prohibition.

Fortunately for the people who work and eat at the restaurants, the spirits in both places seem to be friendly ghosts.

A regular patron of the Greystone is a ghost called Lady Lund, supposedly the wife of the building's original owner, Thomas Lund.

One server who has worked at both restaurants states that the first time she saw Lady Lund was while setting a table at the Greystone. She noticed movement reflected in a wall mirror and saw a woman with long hair and a long robe, gliding along about three feet off the ground.

But as soon as the server turned around, the ghost took off up into a skylight. The server took off too, in the opposite direction—down into the basement, where the manager was doing paperwork. The manager looked up and told the server, "You look like you've just seen a ghost!"

Bingo.

Lady Lund has been witnessed on other occasions as well. One day, Greystone owner Mark Strosahl and his wife, Lori, were serving a private brunch. Lori recalls a woman seated in a red velvet chair in the foyer was posing for a photograph when she suddenly leapt to her feet and ran away from the chair. Lori remembered, "She said she felt something weird and had to get out."

Stranger still was the resulting photo. The woman posing for the photo was wearing a black dress, but the picture showed something blurry and white in the chair. And when the photo was developed, the only recognizable part of the woman was her black shoes. Which makes sense, perhaps, because the sounds of high heels are often heard in the kitchen and hallways of the restaurant—when no human was around to make them.

Some years later, the server who'd seen the good lady disappear through the skylight was starting work at Café Melange. This time, she says, she saw a different spirit. While walking through the swinging doors from the kitchen to the main room, she came upon an old man wearing a narrow-collared shirt. He looked startled and instantly disappeared. When the server ran back into the kitchen to announce what she'd just seen, the cook calmly replied, "Oh, that. That's just Oscar."

Like Lady Lund, he was a regular. Everybody knew Oscar.

Oscar, it seems, is more mischievous than anything. One evening, Kilbourne, the Café Melange's owner, straightened the shades on about a dozen wall lamps in the dining room and then walked into the kitchen. A few seconds later, he walked back out—and all of the shades were askew. Not a little bit—a lot. Oscar had struck.

More than once since then, Kilbourne has heard odd noises. One time, he heard footsteps upstairs when he was in the basement—and when he was alone in the building. Kilbourne ran upstairs, but no one was there. He told a reporter for the *Herald-Republic,* "I was freaked out."

Another restaurant with a spooky presence is the Sports Center, not far away on East Yakima Avenue. Built in 1908, it was originally a hotel and diner called the Columbia. Like so many similar establishments in the Yakima of the early twentieth century, the business saw its share of gambling, bootlegging, and other racy pursuits—including prostitution.

It was on the building's second floor that the latter took place, and it's on the second floor of the present Sports Center where paranormal activity has been reported. Among other things, Sports Center staff members frequently report hearing mysterious clinking glassware and feeling cold spots up there.

It's been suggested that the cause may be the spirit of writer Raymond Carver, a hard-drinking writer who gained fame for his sparse short stories about blue-collar life. Carver grew up in Yakima and used to hang out at the Sports Center. Some people wonder: Is Carver still making his presence felt? Either way, one of the many paranormal research groups that have investigated the situation claims that the Sports Center is one of the most active otherworldly locations in the Pacific Northwest.

Just a few blocks from these haunted restaurants is another place with a spooky history: the Capitol Theatre, once the largest performance hall in the Pacific Northwest. Today restored to its original 1919 glory, it's home to a variety of visiting and local entertainment.

According to legend, it's also home to a ghost named Shorty.

People say that Shorty has been around for sixty years or more. Some speculate that he's the spirit of a stagehand, or perhaps the man who managed the place in the 1930s. According to different versions of the story, this fellow was distraught over the love of an actress or perhaps fearful of losing his job, as motion pictures were gradually causing the death of live vaudeville. In any case, it's said, Shorty committed suicide on the theater's stage.

Today, Shorty has a habit of flicking electrical switches, opening and closing doors, lowering stage curtains, flushing toilets, stealing props, making sound systems cut out, and playing other pranks. He's also able to access—without a ladder, of course—a door twelve feet up that now leads only to a concrete wall. And Shorty also likes to flip the Capitol's 1,500 seats up and down (but only late at night, when all of the audience members are gone). He's also been known to hide items in the catwalk.

All of these pranks are harmless enough, it seems. The theater's technical director, Roger Smith, told a *Herald-Republic* reporter, "He doesn't scare us. This is not a mean ghost. He's just a mischievous ghost."

Shorty is more than just a benign presence; people say that he saved a girl's life, too. According to legend, part of a lighting fixture broke loose high above the stage and was about to hit the girl as she stood below. But the debris changed direction mid-fall and landed harmlessly on the stage. The reason? An intervention by Shorty, of course.

Meanwhile, over at the otherwise innocuous Yakima City Hall, there's an intriguing situation on the third and fourth floors. Up there, the metal grates barring the windows are reminders of a jail that hasn't been used since the 1980s. For several decades after that, the space became storage for extra files and paperwork. Today, it stands mostly empty—except for dozens of metal bunks still in the old, concrete-floored cells.

Could the residents of those cells be behind the stories that city employees tell about the strange events up there— especially the stories about a few of the inmates who died while being detained? Retired police lieutenant Bernie Kline told the *Herald-Republic*, "If there is a ghost, it could be some old alcoholic who liked it up there. City jail kept a lot of them alive. Gave 'em a chance to dry out."

Whether or not the spirits of these jailbirds are responsible for the unexplained events, there have been plenty of reports of otherworldly happenings at City Hall. One long-time city worker (who wants to remain anonymous) recalls moving some boxes to the third floor one evening. She heard footsteps, although she knew she was the only person up there. She looked around the area from which the sounds had come and saw a man sitting by a desk. According to the city worker, the man approached her, then turned and disappeared.

On a different night but in the same place, the same employee encountered another apparent spirit. She told a *Herald-Republic* journalist that the ghost looked disreputable and suspicious—like someone, in short, who would likely have been a jail occupant. When he spotted her, the apparition stood up and began to move aggressively toward her. Not surprisingly, the employee quickly took off in the opposite direction. She later commented, "I don't know enough about ghosts to know if they can hurt you, but I wasn't sticking around to find out."

And then there's the resident ghost of the local parochial school, St. Paul Cathedral School. An administrator at a Yakima youth ministry told a *Herald-Republic* writer, Jane

Gargas, "Everyone who's Catholic knows about the ghost. She lives on."

"She" is Sabina SP, a Sisters of Providence nun who spent almost her entire life as a teacher in the school—and, according to legend, is still around. Apparently, the reason she stays is that she still has a feeling of sentimentality and affection for her longtime home. Gargas comments, "Sabina (or Sister Sabina as she was officially known) can't bear to leave Yakima."

Sister Sabina was one of several Dominican nuns who came to teach at St. Paul's in 1914. She was still active when she died in her eighties. The sister passed away on the school's fourth floor, which was reserved for living quarters.

Sabina was a petite woman, less than five feet tall, but she was respected—or at least feared—for her toughness, especially for her liberal use of a heavy ruler for disciplining students.

Today, Sabina continues to make her presence known. She's allegedly the cause of disturbances such as water stains on the ceiling and the sound of water in restrooms (even when no faucets have been run or toilets flushed). Other signs of her activity from beyond the grave include mysterious handprints on walls, flashing lights, missing items, and windows that bang open and shut for no reason.

The Reverend Robert Siler, an official with the church, told Gargas, perhaps with tongue in cheek, that he has always tried to stay away from the fourth floor, where she died. On a more serious note, Reverend Siler commented on the intersection where his faith meets a belief in spirits of the dead: "We view humans as a composite of flesh and spirit because we were created as both body and soul. So any future life beyond this will be spiritual. . . . There are a lot of things we don't know about this world."

Our look at Yakima's ghost history ends with Old Soldier, the spirit of an ex-military man who, it's been said, once walked the halls of the old Armory at Third and Walnut Streets. (When he served, and hence the type of uniform he wore, is unclear.) The Armory was torn down in 1994 to make way for a new police and legal center, and reports of Old Soldier sightings have largely gone away.

But there's still an unexplained question about the lunches that employees in the new building bring from home. Some of them periodically disappear. . . .

PROSSER

Several spirits—so they say—haunt the beautiful Horse Heaven Hills, in orchard-, wheat-, and grape-rich Benton County southeast of Yakima. Specifically, there have been reports of ghostly activity in the small town of Prosser, the county seat.

According to legend, one of these spirits is a benevolent if mischievous type who haunts the Strand Hotel, which opened in 1910 as the Palace. Over the years the establishment fell into serious disrepair, but in 1985 renovations began to turn it into a bed-and-breakfast catering to visitors—especially those eager to explore the region's wine vineyards.

During the renovation process, it became apparent that there was a resident spirit at the Strand. The manifestations were the usual: doors closed and opened on their own, ghostly footsteps overheard, furniture mysteriously rearranged, items hidden and replaced.

Koni Wallace, who with her husband spearheaded the renovation project, suggested to *Tri-City Herald* reporter Gale Metcalf that the disturbances might have been caused by a former manager of the Strand named Carl. Wallace commented, "When he passed away he didn't have any family, so everything he had is still here. In my kitchen that used to be his kitchen, things will be missing."

Despite being a skeptic, her husband Mike tries to keep his mind open. He told the newspaper's Metcalf, "Sometimes he scares me and sometimes he doesn't. I think he's pretty benevolent from what I can tell."

Among the other ghostly locales in Prosser is Bern's Tavern, one of the oldest establishments of its kind in the state. According to some reports, this historic tavern occasionally plays host to a couple of otherworldly spirits: a cowboy and a sailor in a vintage uniform, who belly up to the bar and melt away if anyone tries to approach them.

And a ghost has made itself apparent in, of all places, a church vicarage—specifically, the home of Debora Jennings, the pastor at St. Matthew's Episcopal Church (now St. Matthews–San Mateo Episcopal Church) in Prosser.

When she was a reporter in 2007 for the *Tri-City Herald*, journalist Elena Olmstead noted that "Debora Jennings knows just how many times the closet door in her guest room has opened on its own—27."

According to Jennings, she hasn't just found that closet door open—she's heard the doorknob jiggle and the latch release. Jennings reports that she's also walked down the stairs to find the pictures on her living room walls at forty-five-degree angles. At first she thought that the strange occurrences were simply part of what came with living in an old house—perhaps the settling of the place's foundations.

But then Pastor Jennings started to notice more strange events. There was the time she found an unexplainable footprint on her bedroom floor. There were the footsteps heard in the hall and the sound of a child crying in her study.

Jennings began to seriously wonder what was going on, and she began to research the history of the vicarage. The pastor learned that the place had been built around 1928, in part above the remains of a previous vicarage that had burned down. Still intrigued, as she told Olmstead, "I began to talk to people in my congregation about the haunted vicarage."

Some members of the congregation urged Pastor Jennings to go public by contacting the producers of a cable show, *Ghost Hunters,* which investigates paranormal events. She did, and the TV people, intrigued, assembled a team to investigate. As part of their hunt for ghosts in the vicarage, members of the team asked aloud if something was in the closet. They later asserted that they heard three taps in answer, and they also reported that they heard what sounded like the voice of a little girl humming in the guest room closet.

The pastor remarked to Olmstead, the newspaper reporter, that the whole experience had been a positive and thought-provoking one for her as a member of the clergy. Although she takes it all lightly, it gave Jennings the chance to discuss with her congregation serious ideas about ghosts, angels, and other spiritual mysteries. The results of any specific paranormal investigations, she noted, were in her opinion just secondary considerations. She commented, "For me the important piece of all of this was to be able to engage in a conversation with our young people."

Talk about a holy ghost!

MOSES LAKE

North of Benton County, nestled in the dry landscape of Grant County, is the small town of Moses Lake. (By the way, despite the fact that a number of its early settlers were Presbyterian missionaries, Moses Lake's name comes not from the Biblical character but from a local Native American chief.)

A few completely unsubstantiated legends have been noted there, but reporter Sarah Kehoe chronicled what is Moses Lake's most intriguing ghostly tale in a 2010 piece for the *Columbia Basin Herald*.

According to Kehoe's article, three-year-old Malaki Juarez was having fun in his grandmother's house with his mom, Martha Juarez, taking pictures with her camera. She told Kehoe, "My son loves taking pictures on any camera he can get his hands on. He only takes a picture when he sees something. Something has to catch his attention."

That something, she believes, was a ghost.

After going home and putting Malaki to bed, Martha Juarez scrolled through her camera's photos, deleting blurry mistakes, until she came to the last one, which her son had shot in a hallway that was bare because it was in the process of being remodeled.

"I noticed there were figures in this picture," Juarez recalled, "and at first I thought it was a lamp or maybe the light hit it weird. But the closer I looked I saw what appeared to be three people. I showed my boyfriend and he noticed the people looked like the ghost from the movie *Scream*."

As Martha zoomed in to see the picture more closely, she thought she discerned three things: a white-faced figure dressed in a black cloak, a dark-faced figure of the same height dressed in white, and a small figure dressed in black with a white face.

The couple tried to debunk the picture by taking several photos in the same location, turning the lights on and off. But the photos seemed distinctly different, and Martha Juarez was convinced: "I think my son captured something we can't see."

The next day Martha showed the picture to her son and asked him who the people were. He replied, "Those are my friends," and identified one of them as being named Mike.

Martha told Kehoe, "It freaked me out. My son is young, but he is very precise. He calls things by name and has always been very detailed when talking about events or people."

Furthermore, Juarez says, the snapping of the ghostly photo wasn't Malaki's first brush with paranormal activity. She stated, "My son is weird. He talks to walls as if there are people in front of them. He's been doing this since my mom moved into her house and he only does it at her house." In that house, the family says, there have been a number of spooky events over time. Martha recalled, "One of my sisters lives in a yellow room and this room freaks us out the most. At night we always hear chuckling, rattling noises, and scratching noises. . . . We all have that eerie feeling, that feeling you get when you know something is just not right, you know? You just don't feel comfortable." Martha's sister Margarita agrees, citing a time when she woke up to find that the phone in the room had moved quite far away from its normal spot, apparently by itself.

Martha Juarez says that she's now a believer. She told Kehoe, "It's creepy, but I'd really like to know what's going on. I am a believer of ghosts and think they hang out for a reason. They watch us, protect us, or simply have nowhere else to go because of life choices. I think technology can capture things the eye cannot see and when there is no explanation, it's time to explore."

WENATCHEE

Wenatchee, the seat of Chelan County, is on the Columbia River and close to the rugged mountains that divide the state—well situated, in other words, for water- and snow-sports aficionados.

Not to mention those who might be interested in the paranormal.

A building near the corner of Miller and Fifth Streets, now a charming bed-and-breakfast called the Ivy Wild Inn, is a case in point. It's said that a woman who once lived in the building was somewhat less than virtuous—actually, she regularly cheated on her husband while he was traveling for business.

One day he returned unexpectedly, caught his wife in bed with a lover, and killed her in a rage. (The fate of the lover is unclear.) It's said that the cuckolded husband can still be heard walking up and down the stairs repeatedly, reliving his dark deed.

Unfortunately, this may be just a story. Reporter Michele Mihalovich of the *Wenatchee World* investigated the rumor in 2009 and found it unverifiable. Not only that, she couldn't find anyone who had felt the presence of something other-worldly—or at least anyone who would admit to it. When Mihalovich asked for details from a woman whose family owned the place during the 1960s and 1970s, the former occupant was shocked: "What? No one was ever murdered in that house. That was just a story me and my husband used to tell our kids to scare them. It's just a story we made up."

(Which raises an interesting question: Who would tell their kids a story about a grisly murder and flagrant adultery occurring in their home?)

Mihalovich went further in her investigations, asking current Ivy Wild owner Ashley Kitos if she had ever noticed anything spooky. The reporter writes, "So how many times in the three years of owning the bed and breakfast has Ashley Kitos heard the husband walking up the stairs to the bedroom that torments his soul?

"'Never,' she said. 'I have people who are writing books and calling me all the time asking about it. But in the three years we've owned it absolutely nothing weird has ever happened.'"

Oh well. It makes a good story. Unless, maybe, you're a little kid who is being told about grisly murder and flagrant adultery. . . .

MISSION RIDGE

High in the Cascades west of Wenatchee is the popular skiing, snowboarding, and hiking resort of Mission Ridge, the site of a longstanding legend about a wartime bomber crash and a pilot who apparently still wanders the site . . . with a bloody propeller plunged into his chest.

Visitors to the site, which is in the Squilchuck Basin, can see a memorial to the World War II incident—a bomber wing and a plaque. Adventurous souls can even hike around the area, looking for remnants of the crash. The plaque, placed there by the Veterans of Foreign Wars and a local Eagle Scout troop, tells the story:

On a stormy night of September 30, 1944, Flight Crew 22, on a training mission from Walla Walla Army Air Base, found itself off course and lost above the rugged Cascade Mountain Range. They were flying a B-24 "Liberator" Heavy Bomber. The

night was rainy and the valley was enshrouded
with heavy fog. Around 8:00 p.m. the Beehive
Lookout reported hearing the drone of a plane's
engines as it passed directly overhead. Within moments a fire was seen faintly illuminating the fog,
alerting the lookout that the plane had probably
crashed. Due to the darkness, weather, and terrain, search efforts were delayed. The next morning when a rescue party reached this rocky bowl,
just 500 feet below the crest of Mission Ridge,
they found the flames had been extinguished by
the heavy rainfall from the previous night. Pieces
of the wreckage were strewn hundreds of yards
across the slope and the bodies of all six crewmembers were found. There were no survivors.

The bodies of the airmen and some parts of the wreckage, including the plane's machine guns, were carried off
the mountain in a horse pack train. Since then, however,
the story goes that the spirit of one of the dead aviators,
complete with his grisly injury, has been spotted wandering
around the rugged terrain.

Quoted in 2009 by *Wenatchee World* reporter Mihalovich,
Mark Milliette, then the general manager of Mission Ridge
Ski and Board Resort, commented that he first heard about
the Prop Man while sitting around a campfire as a Boy Scout:
"You'll hear people talking about seeing him when they were
hiking or skiing. People have seen him year-round."

But Milliette also joked to Mihalovich that some reports
have come from skiers relaxing in the bar of Mission Ridge's
lodge after a day out on the mountain. It seems that the
Prop Man likes to sneak up on people and scare their ski

boots off—thus providing a handy excuse when they wipe out on the slopes.

LEAVENWORTH

Another ghostly legend related in the 2009 Mihalovich article comes from the Bavarian-themed town of Leavenworth, on Highway 2 west of Mission Ridge. For this piece, reporter Mihalovich interviewed Sandy Owens-Carmody, owner of Leavenworth's Tumwater Inn Restaurant. Mihalovich wrote, "Owens-Carmody said she accidentally acquired a little girl ghost when she purchased an 1891 piano from the Douglas General Store east of Waterville." (Waterville is the seat of Douglas County.)

Owens-Carmody also told the reporter that a woman named Cat Stevens (no, not *that* Cat Stevens) from the west side of the Cascades visits the Tumwater Inn regularly because the piano belonged to her when she was little. The restaurant owner stated, "She told me it was haunted even back then."

Not just that: Owens-Carmody also says that a stubborn spirit named Ruby Smith has been sensed in her place. Ruby, according to this story, likes to move photographs and glasses in the bar area. Sometimes she sips coffee at a table and stares out the window at what used to be a car lot owned by her late husband. She's been known to move objects around—and once attacked Owens-Carmody with a cleaning product! The restaurant owner commented, "Sometimes when I'm restocking the linen closet, stuff just flies off the shelves. And the other day she hit me three times in the head with a Lysol can. . . . [Y]ou can feel her presence and smell her perfume."

ELLENSBURG

Ellensburg, the seat of Kittitas County, is north of Yakima and on the other side of the Cascades from Seattle. A lovely town, Ellensburg has a number of restored nineteenth-century brick buildings. Perhaps not surprisingly, Ellensburg also has a long and rich history of hauntings.

Milton Wagy, the reference librarian of the Ellensburg Public Library and an expert on local history, says he often gets requests for information—especially about strange events in private homes. Quoted in the *Kittitas County Daily Record* in 2007, Wagy commented, "I do a lot of house research—scores and scores of houses—and most of the time if the person coming in wants to know about the history of their house, usually if they're under 25, I'll say, 'Let me guess, you think it's haunted!' and they say, 'Yes!' . . . I help people obtain information about the houses they live in. There are some houses that are 120 years old and a lot of people have lived there—and some may have died there and in some cases it might be gruesome."

One story about a private home begins with two sisters, Clareta and Leta, members of a prominent pioneer family, the Olmsteads. According to legend, their ghosts can still be detected in the Dutch-style house on the corner of Chestnut and Washington, which was once theirs.

Linda Kapoi, her daughter Mende Dias, and Dias's young sons moved into the house in 2003. The plan was to start a restaurant and tearoom. But they began to have second thoughts when strange things began to happen within their first few nights in the home.

The first time something happened, Dias came downstairs from her bedroom pale, to tell her family about a startling experience. In a 2003 article by Andrea Pascoe of the *Ellensburg Daily Record*, Kapoi recalls, "She said she felt like someone was standing over her while she was in bed. She felt a presence and saw a figure. She asked me to come up and have a look. I didn't see anything."

But several more experiences led Dias to believe that something supernatural was going on. In particular, she saw one especially notable ghost. Pascoe writes that, according to Dias, the apparition was "a very proper woman outfitted in a black Edwardian-style dress with a high white collar. The woman had dark eyes and hair and wore a stern expression on her face. Though not menacing, the woman would simply stand and look down on Dias as she slept."

Then another member of the family had an otherworldly experience. A few nights after Dias spotted the lady dressed in black, Kapoi put her young grandson Max to bed. When she came back downstairs, she relates, she heard clapping and laughter coming from Max's room. She hurried upstairs and saw the boy standing on the bed, giggling and talking as if he were speaking to someone in the room. He repeated "No, no, no!" in a delighted voice and hopped backward toward the bedstead.

When Kapoi turned on the light, Max rubbed his eyes and began to cry. He told his grandmother that he was playing with the ladies, and that they were now in the bedroom closet because the light had scared them. Kapoi says she put the boy back to bed and shrugged off the incident as nothing more than an overactive imagination.

But a few weeks later Kapoi had a change of heart, after she had a spooky encounter of her own. She was getting ready for bed in her downstairs bedroom, she told the newspaper. The door was slightly open, and Kapoi saw the shadow of a man, dressed in an old Army uniform, pass by. She followed him through the house: "He walked by in the living room toward the stairs. That was the last I saw of him."

The two women contacted Wagy, the librarian. In a conversation with this author, Wagy stated that he was able to tell the family that their home had once belonged to the Olmstead sisters, Clareta and Leta.

The sisters, Wagy says, had been raised on the family farm and later attended Ellensburg Normal School (now Central Washington University) to become teachers. While in school, they and their grandmother lived in the family's house on Washington Street, the one later occupied by Dias and Kapoi.

According to legend, the sisters still live in the Washington Street house—in spirit form, of course. It's unclear where the ghost in the old Army uniform comes from.

Pascoe writes, "Once Kapoi and Dias learned of their rental home's rich history, they gracefully accepted the occasional visits from the spirits." They also confirmed their hunch that the women Max played with were the Olmstead sisters. When they showed Max a photo of Clareta and Leta, he said that they were "his ladies."

In time, Dias and Kapoi learned to make their peace, of sorts, with the ghostly presences in their home. But the family did make a few adjustments to accommodate their supernatural housemates. Notably, Dias moved her bed to the other side of her room, so that any spirits who were there could look out the window easily. But she says that she never felt a ghostly presence after that, and six months later the family moved out.

Meanwhile, there have been reports that Clareta and Leta—or perhaps some other departed soul—may be haunting the old homestead. When the sisters inherited the family farm—which by now encompassed some five hundred acres—they donated it to the state. Today it is Olmstead Place State Park.

State Park Ranger Brandon Hoekstra lived in the park when *Ellensburg Daily Record* reporter Mary Swift interviewed him in 2009. Hoekstra told her that a lot of people show up looking for ghosts in the park. He'd never seen any such thing himself, he reported, although he admits that there have been some unexplained events.

There was the time the alarm system went off for no reason, for instance. He has also heard tales told by a number of visitors to the park about sensing an otherworldly presence. The ranger commented, "I don't completely believe in this stuff. But people do come in asking about it because this place is listed as being haunted. I really haven't felt too much—but a lot of other people have."

Specifically, he told Swift, there have been reports about the spirits of the park's namesakes, the Olmstead family, in the farmhouse that is still standing on park grounds. Hoekstra commented, "The family lived there until 1981 when the last sister, Leta May, died. I've heard people say there's, like, a presence in the farmhouse." A display in one of the vintage buildings may fuel the ongoing speculation about the place, because one of the objects there is an old Ouija board—a device used to try to contact the dead.

The story of the Olmstead house is by no means Ellensburg's only ghostly legend. Consider, for example, the grisly tale of two lynched men and their spirits.

Back in 1894, Ellensburg (like the rest of the region) was a pretty rough-and-tumble place. One August night, down on Third Street, a man named Sam Vinson drunkenly accosted another man, John Buerglin, in a tavern and demanded that

Buerglin buy him a drink. A quarrel ensued: Buerglin was stabbed and Vinson was severely beaten.

While the fight was going on, Sam Vinson's son Charles arrived, armed with a revolver. A fourth man, Michael Kohlepp, tried to stop him but the younger man fired and shot Kohlepp in the chest. The wounded man died a few hours later, and Buerglin succumbed to his injury a few days later.

A number of Ellensburg's men felt that the Vinsons would be acquitted during a trial. Historian Mary Virginia Kern wrote, "[S]oon there was strong talk of lynching both of the men by those who wished justice to be meted out to them for the crime they had committed, and also because the two men killed were very popular with the Dutch colony in the valley."

The evening of August 13, the day that Buerglin died, the streets were crowded with armed men seeking justice— or at least revenge. The sheriff and six guards stood duty at the courthouse to protect the Vinsons from the mob, and the keys to the courthouse and jail were entrusted to F. D. Schnebly, a respected local resident. But the mob broke down the door, forced the lawmen on guard duty to surrender, and tried to take the keys from Schnebly. He told them that they would have to kill him first, which they declined to do. Instead, they spent two hours battering down the jailhouse door.

The senior and junior Vinsons were then led, with ropes around their necks, to the home of George Dickson. Dickson begged the mob not to hang them in his yard, because his wife was seriously ill. The mob then led their prisoners to a tree on the corner of Seventh and Pine. Kern wrote, "The fire bell was ringing and whistles were screeching, and with their thirst for the lives of the two Vinson men, father and son, they were beyond any reason."

Asked if they had any last words, Sam Vinson kept quiet, but his son professed his love for his mother. Then they were hung from a tall tree.

Justice was not served in the aftermath of this horrifying tale. Some of the men in the mob that evening were tried, and a few convicted, but in time all of them avoided punishment.

But that was hardly the end of the story. That fall, Kern's mother was returning home from a visit with friends. Kern noted, "It was a dark night in early fall, so dark that you could hardly see your hand before your face. Just as Mother arrived under the 'lynching tree' she heard scream upon scream. Her heart fairly stopped as she was not used to being out alone, especially on such a dark night."

As time went on, many other people reported seeing something strange at the tree. Some claimed it was eight feet tall, but some said even taller. All agreed it was a shadowy figure that made a strange shuffling noise as it walked back and forth. It was known to walk across the street, facing the house of the Fogarty family as Mrs. Fogarty waited for her husband to arrive home from their farm.

Then someone plucked up the courage to follow the apparition when it shuffled off. Seven blocks away, it entered a ruined house. The witness saw a young farm hand inside, taking off a long black veil that reached from the top of his stovepipe hat to his waist. Then he took off the rest of his outfit—a woman's black dress and a pair of shoes with loose soles. When confronted, the young man admitted that he just wanted to scare people.

So it was apparently a hoax. Or was it . . . ? Perhaps there is something to the idea that the spirits of the two wrongly hanged men still roam the area. In any case, the story of the corner of Seventh and Pine is a disturbing tale—and a good ghost story.

And then there's Lola, the resident ghost in Kamola Hall, on the campus of Central Washington University in Ellensburg. Kamola is the second oldest building on the CWU campus, completed in 1920. In 2011, Alea Thorne, a reporter for the *Observer,* the CWU newspaper, commented, "[I]f someone decides to stay [overnight] they may run into Kamola's friendly ghost or at least experience unexplainable happenings."

These reported events include footsteps on the roof in the middle of the night and knocking on doors—all happening when no one is around. And there have been reports of music emanating from a computer that mysteriously started to play by itself. Furthermore, in Thorne's article student Stephen Candeleria commented that the building's resident advisors (RAs) were checking the halls during a fire drill one night when they supposedly saw a ghost they nicknamed "Lola Kamola." They say she was wearing a white dress.

A photographer who works for the school, Richard Villacres, once had his own encounter with Lola. In 2002, Villacres conducted a photo shoot in the Kamola Hall attic with a woman modeling a 1940s-era wedding dress. The assignment was not remarkable—until Villacres developed his film, and what he saw made his blood run cold. He told Thorne, "I shot three rolls of film inside Kamola of my model, and of the three rolls of film that I shot inside—two of them came out black, nothing—which has never, ever happened to me."

Even more remarkable was what the photographer found on the third roll: "The one roll that came out had all kinds of bizarre fogging and weird marks on it. Especially one that was taken in the hallway inside. There is this ghostly figure in the background—all this weird effect is on there. I had no explanation for that."

Other film that Villacres shot that day, outside the dorm, turned out normally, and a check by the film manufacturer found nothing amiss with the mysterious rolls. Nor could any sign of malfunction be found in Villacres's camera. He took the same camera out on another shoot, and again, everything was working perfectly. Villacres's conclusion: "She screwed with my film, and, honestly, I have no explanation for it. Something weird happened."

There are several versions of the legend behind Lola. Becky Watson, the director of the university's public relations and marketing, told Thorne, "There's all different kinds of speculation with Lola, how she has arrived or may have arrived at Kamola. There's [theories] that she just showed up after being gone or she may have committed suicide. No one really knows the true story."

According to one version of the tale, Lola lived in Kamola early in the twentieth century, when the school was still Washington Normal School, a teacher's college. (The name was changed in 1937.) But when Lola's sweetheart was killed during World War I, she was so despondent that she hung herself from the rafters of her room on the fourth floor. (Another version was that the love of Lola's life died during a different world war, in the 1940s.)

Quoted in a column by J. Scott Wilson, who writes for a website maintained by Tampa Bay TV station MORtv, a contributor named T. R. Talbott commented:

> My son lived in Kamola Hall, a large dorm on the Central Washington University campus, in Ellensburg, Wash. . . .

After a few weeks, he and his roommate (an Eagle Scout, and just about as boring a person as you could ever hope to meet) began to notice the sound of someone moving stuff across the floor directly above their room, sort of a "Drag, drag, scrape, THUMP" sound.

They got tired of getting their sleep disturbed, but didn't want to anger a possible upperclassman, so they asked the building manager who lived above them. "No one," he replied, adding that the fourth floor had been sealed off since the 1960s and that NO ONE had lived there in a very very long time.

After some more investigation, the boys found out about "Lola Kamola."

She had been a student at what was then the state Teachers College. This was just at the beginning of WWI. She was madly in love with a fellow student, and he went away to war. Despondent, she then hung herself in her fourth floor room. That room was directly above my son's room.

Eventually, the boys learned to just talk to the ghost as if it were a living person, asking it to stop moving around and making noise, when they did so, the sound ALWAYS stopped, and would not resume until the following night. My son lived in that room for two years total; his roommate moved however.

Meanwhile, the Ellensburg Public Library may have its own ghost. The library's longtime director, Celeste Kline, passed away in 2005. Ted Barkley, the Ellensburg city manager at the time, told the *Daily Record*, "She was the heart and soul of the Ellensburg Public Library. She was relentless in her passion for that library."

Wagy, the reference librarian, commented in a conversation with this author that some people have reported strange events at the library since Kline's departure. This has led to speculation that her spirit lingers and still roams the stacks. Calling her "an incredibly powerful micromanager," Wagy remarked, "Celeste would roll over in her grave if she knew she didn't have control of the library."

Maybe she is, indeed, rolling over in her grave. And maybe she's still out there—sort of.

ROSLYN

East of the Cascades on I-90 is the small town of Roslyn, known to many as the place where the quirky TV series *Northern Exposure* was filmed in the early 1990s. It wasn't a spooky show—but despite the relatively harmless nature of *Northern Exposure,* Roslyn's best-known cultural export, the town still has some haunting stories to tell.

(By the way, for a TV show that really *was* spooky, check out *Twin Peaks*, much of which was filmed in North Bend and Snoqualmie, on the other side of the mountains.)

As for Roslyn: "It's a place steeped in history—and home to memories mined over more than a century," reporter Mary Swift wrote in the *Ellensburg Daily Record* in 2007. "Roslyn's iconic Brick saloon, built in 1889, also may be home to something else: ghosts."

The bar, located on Pennsylvania Avenue, lays claim to the title of oldest continuously operated saloon in the state. Quoted in Swift's article, manager Larry Najar commented, "We had a bartender quit once because he got so freaked out. He was alone. He just ran out of there. We've had people say they've seen ghosts—a little girl, a cowboy.

We've heard that more than once. And there's a piano back-stage in the other room that has played by itself."

Najar remarked that he has had his own slightly spooky encounter. He once took an armful of pool cues downstairs, put them on a table, and steadied them to keep them from rolling. When he came back soon after, they were standing against the wall and the table, apparently having moved themselves.

Some say that the 2 R Bar and Bistro, located in a nearly ninety-year-old building on First Street, is also haunted. The bar's owners, Ronda and Ray Thompson, will tell you that . . . well, things happen. Quoted in a 2009 *Ellensburg Daily Record* article, again by Mary Swift, Ronda Thompson stated, "Weird things. Glasses have disappeared since day one. And we've heard things upstairs where there's a vacant apartment."

There have also been reports at the 2 R of the ghostly presence of two men—a gambler and a miner, to go by their looks—lingering in the bar. And the eerie appearance of a young girl, clad in an apron, as well as a short, bald man who walks with a cane. Both the girl and the short man have been seen upstairs, according to legend.

Swift adds that the inexplicable events don't end there:

More than once . . . the smell of cigarette smoke
has lingered on the main floor even though Thompson is a non-smoker who opened her business as
a non-smoking establishment even before the law
required it. And then, there was the fire—started
by a candle left on the bar—that burned part of
the bar top and then just "went out."

Fortunate coincidence? Thompson doesn't think so. "I'm thinking somebody's watching this place," she says. . . . "I've never felt threatened or intimidated. It was just comforting to know whenever [any apparitions] are here they're having a good time."

Chapter 12

Eastern and Southeastern Washington

Eastern and Southeastern Washington are often thought of as being every part of the state east of the Cascade Mountains—the Cascade Curtain, as it's sometimes called to differentiate the west and east, which are widely different in climate, political leanings, and much more. (They're so different, in fact, that there are periodic calls for the eastern half of the state to split off and become independent.)

For our purposes, however, Eastern and Southeastern Washington include counties Ferry, Stevens, Pend Oreille (if you don't already know how to pronounce this, impress your friends by calling it "Pondoray"), Lincoln, Spokane, Adams, Whitman, Franklin, Walla Walla, Columbia, Garfield, and Asotin. These sparsely populated but starkly beautiful regions enjoy dry, sunny conditions— about eight inches of rain a year is typical—and rich farmland.

Visitors interested in unusual destinations should not only check out the region's ghostly attractions. Eastern Washington is also home to such amazing places as the Stonerose fossil site, near the Ferry County town of Republic on the region's northern border, where you can see and even dig in the rich fossil remains from fifty million years ago.

STEVENS HALL AT WASHINGTON STATE UNIVERSITY

Washington State University in Pullman began life in 1890 as Washington Agricultural College and School of Science.

Today, Wazzu (as it's known to its friends) is the second-largest university in the state. A number of strange stories have been reported on campus, several of them revolving around Stevens Hall, built in 1895 and today one of the oldest buildings on campus. It was a women's dorm in those days and remains so now.

According to *Our Story*, a website maintained by the students and faculty of the university, in 1971 a team of custodians was performing its regular routine of cleaning the dorms before the new session began, and Stevens Hall was the last building on the list.

Coming in the front door, the custodians noticed that a big chunk of carpet, about five feet by six feet, was missing. The cleaning crew chalked it up to nothing more sinister than vandalism. They started through their usual cleaning process, but when they came to one room they were in for a horrifying surprise—one wall in the far corner of the room was splattered with blood.

The subsequent police investigation was able to establish a link between the blood spatters and a missing-persons case that had remained unsolved. This mysterious disappearance involved a WSU student who had left the campus for her summer break but had never arrived home.

The police investigating the disappearance had been stymied—until three months later, when a road crew working on the side of the highway near Lewiston, Idaho, found the girl's body. It was wrapped up—in the piece of carpet missing from Stevens's front hallway seen by the cleaning crew. Because no one had been in the dorm over break, the missing carpet and the blood-spattered room had gone unnoticed.

At the time the body had been discovered, a rumor had circulated that the notorious serial killer Ted Bundy was responsible for the murder—a rumor that proved to be false. Still, the terrifying case of the murdered girl, the piece of carpet, and the blood-spattered room remains unsolved.

Since then, there have been further strange events reported by the residents of Stevens Hall, especially those who live in basement rooms. These students have complained regularly about strange noises, doors that open and shut by themselves, eerie screams, and other otherworldly occurrences.

Could they be connected to the horrific, unsolved crime of 1971?

This story is fairly recent. But another one, dating from an earlier time, is by far the strangest and most enduring legend about Stevens: the tale of the black cat.

During its early decades, the late nineteenth and early twentieth centuries, Stevens Hall was the school's social hub as well as a women's dormitory. As such, it was a popular location for social events such as dances, teas, and story readings. This last activity was especially popular in the days before television and even radio. One enduring tradition was that every Halloween Edgar Allan Poe's short story "The Black Cat" was read aloud to a group of students at Stevens Hall.

This classic horror story, first published in 1843, is told by a condemned man confessing his crimes. It seems that he and his wife had, among their many pets, a huge black cat. The story goes on to relate how the man, in a drunken rage, tortured and hanged his once-beloved cat. Racked with guilt, he adopted a similar-looking cat but, in a terrifying series of events, the cat caused him to murder his wife and hide her behind a basement wall. As the police investigated this crime, the basement wall collapsed, revealing the woman's body—with the screaming black cat on her head.

No one knows why this particular horror story was chosen for Stevens Hall's annual Halloween read-aloud, but chosen it was. And for many years, it remained just that—a tradition of reading a shivery story out loud.

But in time it became something more. The annual reading evolved into a widespread rumor that on Halloween a terrifying, ferocious, and unnaturally large black cat stalked Stevens Hall. It was said that this oversize feline could be spotted roaming outside the building and in its corridors, leaving in its path a trail of eerie and sometimes evil sensations.

Over the years, a number of people, students and faculty alike, have reported that they witnessed something strange and spine-tingling as they walked toward Stevens Hall late at night. As they approached the building, they said, they would be startled by a sudden whisking sound and a dimly perceived shape or shadow of some kind of creature. This unidentifiable animal would quickly vanish into the night, disappearing into a gap under the front porch. Some witnesses also reported that when they went closer to investigate they could see two bright spots, glimpsed far back under the vine-covered porch.

At the same time, these witnesses reported, they felt "a strange prickling sensation. . . . Occasionally, a couple returning late at night to the west entrance . . . could see between the porch vines two shining orbs like coals of fire, which left the shivering pair in uncertainty whether the phosphorescence came from the eyes of the legendary black cat that dwelt under the house." (This quote, and the other quotes in this account, are from an essay, date unknown, that recounts the legend in appropriately spooky, old-fashioned, and purple prose.)

At Washington State College, as it was called in those days, lights went out all over the campus at 10:30 p.m. There was no way to turn the electricity back on, so candles and lanterns were the only illumination possible late in the evening. Sometimes residents of Stevens Hall reported that during these dark nights they could hear a piercing cry from outside their windows, "at once plaintive, sorrowful and full of longing, as though it were uttered in the hope of a far-off response from some lost but sympathetic soul." The scream sounded as though it could have come from a human, they said—or, perhaps, from a sinister black cat.

Throwing their windows open, the apprehensive but curious women would peer out into the night, trying to locate the source of the chilling sound. But nothing was ever seen or heard beyond that single anguished cry.

Variations on this theme were passed down from year to year and from generation to generation of new students. In fact, there was a tradition in the dorm of introducing the chilling legend to these students as they sat in a circle in one of the rooms in Stevens, illuminated only by candlelight.

Sometimes the legend was used as a cautionary tale for students who flouted the dorm curfew hours. These miscreants, who insisted on sneaking in or out when they should have been safely tucked in bed, were solemnly warned that they ran the possibility of running into the gigantic black cat if they continued to leave the dorm or return to it in the middle of the night.

SUSANNE

The persistent legend of the black cat is not the only eerie story connected to Stevens Hall. Depending on the version of another story you hear, another eerie bit of the dormitory's lore may or may not be linked to the legendary black cat.

This is the tale of poor Susanne. At some point in the early decades of Wazzu, Susanne was a resident of Stevens Hall. They say she was tall, with thick dark hair, pale skin, and thoughtful, ink-black eyes. She was also a little strange and standoffish, rarely participating in activities with the other residents of the dormitory. It was said that once or twice a male student came to visit her, but the only one who ever saw this mysterious visitor was the dormitory's preceptress (as the resident dorm mother was called in those days). She told students that he was a handsome lad, but she also noted that there was something strange and otherworldly about his eyes.

For some reason or other, the preceptress was rather hard on Susanne, perhaps because of her standoffish behavior. More than once, the dorm mother called Susanne to her room and delivered a stern lecture. None of the other residents knew what went on during these interviews.

One day, however, one of the Stevens girls literally bumped into Susanne after one such session ended, as Susanne was leaving the preceptress's office. This student couldn't help but notice that Susanne's eyes were red; evidently, she had been crying. Susanne was so preoccupied that she did not notice anyone was even outside the office until she collided with the other student. Susanne mumbled, "Beg pardon," and hastened on her way.

The next day, one of the students, noticing that the strange student was not around, asked the Stevens preceptress where Susanne was. The matter-of-fact reply was, "Susanne went home today. Her folks sent for her. There seems to be trouble in the family. I hardly think she will be back this semester."

A reasonable explanation—and there matters would no doubt have rested had it not been for a newspaper article that one of the Stevens residents noticed. The news had originated in a remote part of the state, where Susanne had grown up. It seems that the young woman had disappeared shortly after returning to her hometown from school—and that no trace of her had been found. A thorough search was made, and the police checked nearby railway stations to see if she could have left the area, but without success.

Soon after this newspaper article was noticed and passed around, one of the residents of Stevens Hall met a man who happened to come from Susanne's part of the state. He said that he was familiar with the circumstances of the incident. He further stated that it was indeed very mysterious. But he also hinted in a dark voice that he believed, if inanimate things could talk, investigating a cold, deep lake near his home could throw light on the matter. But this search was never undertaken, and Susanne never did turn up.

According to the essay in *Our Story* written about the legend of the black cat, somehow the stories of the cat and Susanne became intertwined. The essay continues, "How the imagination of the one girl in the Hall who said that the black cat story always reminded her of poor Susanne could ever have led her to see any connection between two things so utterly unlike, is [unclear]; but no sooner had it been suggested than it sank into the life of the Hall, and never was the one mentioned without thought of the other flashing upon the mind."

The stories grew and grew over the years, and in time Susanne, the mysterious feline specter of Stevens Hall, or both were invoked whenever anything unusual occurred.

For example, strange reports have been made by a number of students who have roomed on the second floor, at the south end of the dorm near the stairway. They say they have heard soft steps, as if someone—perhaps a woman?—could be climbing the stairway from the hall below and continuing on to the attic. No matter how intensely the students listened, however, they could never hear anything other than those soft steps.

But some people wondered what the origin of the strange sounds could be. Might they be coming from the legendary, mysterious black cat prowling around?

Even stranger, there have been a number of other eerie incidents involving the attic in Stevens Hall. This storage space has since been remodeled and divided into sections, but in the early days it was simply one large room. Only a rough floor had been laid, and there were many dark nooks and cobwebbed corners where forgotten or neglected items were stashed. Trunks and boxes were piled high in these corners, along with discarded mattresses, broken-down rocking chairs, and similar items.

It is likely that among these piles of junk were Susanne's mattress and other furniture. No one was eager to claim them, as she disappeared so mysteriously.

Over time, the students who lived in Stevens Hall sometimes had occasion to go up to the attic, to retrieve an item from a trunk, or to put something away until the end of the term. A number of the students who ventured up there reported hearing strange things, such as their own footsteps resounding at unusually loud volumes—far louder than would have been expected. Because of these eerie experiences, many students were scared to go into the attic by themselves. If they had no choice, they certainly did not stay any longer than was necessary before hurrying back to their rooms.

The essay reprinted in *Our Story* relates one especially dreadful incident experienced by a group of students who ventured into the attic: "One night when the wind was shrieking through the chinks in the attic like a concert of lost souls, there was a crash in the attic, as of something falling, followed by a tramp, tramp, tramp, as of a person walking heavily across the attic floor."

Several of the young women asleep on the second floor awoke with a start, and as the heavy tread continued it startled them into a state of fearful wakefulness. Lighting a pair of candles, two of the bravest women hurried down to the bedroom of the preceptress. Other students, less bold, followed them down, clothed only in their nightgowns. They informed the preceptress that there seemed to be a man in the dorm—something that was strictly forbidden except for supervised visits during the day—and that several of the students had distinctly heard him walking across the attic floor.

The preceptress took a broom in hand and led a procession up the north stairway to the attic. She was skeptical, attributing the reports to nothing more than the students' active imaginations, but she was willing to humor them by investigating.

When the group reached the attic, the door was slightly ajar—unlatched, but not open. After a moment of breathless suspense, the preceptress quietly pushed the door open with her broom.

Without warning, high in the air above the heads of everyone, a terrifying black object shot out—something alive and furious. The essay continues, "[I]ts eyeballs of fire, its four legs spread wide and its long black tail of enormous size, with furious spits and growls, [it] landed on the first platform [of the stairs], and, now on this side, now on that, with scratch and scramble and redoubled spits and yawls flew down the stairway."

Not surprisingly, the astonished students—and the preceptress—were scared stiff, and they fled as quickly as they could. As the young women made their panicked way down from the attic, a series of bloodcurdling shrieks pierced the air and the bizarre black spirit flew above them.

And then the apparition was gone, as suddenly as it had appeared.

All of the students' candles had been dropped in the confusion, and even if they had been still available there were no matches to relight them. Nor was there a telephone in the hallway in those days. As a result, the pandemonium took place in total darkness and with no chance of contacting anyone from the outside. But somehow they made it. Tremblingly, the students, still in their nightgowns, crept back to their rooms and, shivering, crawled into bed for what was surely a sleepless night.

The next day, a custodian was asked to seal off every opening in the porch and install a better lock on the attic door. He did so—during the daytime, of course—while keeping a sharp eye out for anything strange. But he saw nothing, and the black cat was never seen or heard of again—except in the eerie stories that have continued to be part of the tradition of Stevens Hall.

MORE GHOSTS AT WSU

By no means is the weird tale of the black cat of Stevens Hall the only ghostly legend to persist in making the rounds at Washington State University. For example, over on the twelfth floor of Orton Hall, another one of the campus's dormitories, a fellow named Railroad Sam is said to be in residence.

According to legend, Railroad Sam is a benign (although dead) entity who lives on the twelfth floor of the building. His nickname, so they say, was inspired by his fondness for standing alone by one of the dorm's windows and watching the trains go by as they chugged through town.

Speculation is rife as to why Sam has chosen Orton as his favorite spot. Was he a former student who once lived there? Did one of his children live there as a student? Or did he choose Orton simply because there's a great view of the trains from its upper floors?

Who's to say?

Railroad Sam doesn't always make his presence felt. (Maybe this is because Orton is a relatively modern building. Otherworldly spirits do seem to prefer older structures, after all.) A more prominent example of a ghostly presence, one that has been reported many times, can be found over at venerable Bryan Hall, one of the campus's oldest buildings and today the home of Wazzu's music and drama departments.

There are several resident owls in Bryan's clock tower, and although they're quite normal, perhaps their slightly eerie demeanor signals the number of spooky stories that persist around Bryan Hall. Far spookier than owls in the belfry, however, are the stories told about Enoch A. Bryan, who from 1893 to 1915 was president of what was then the Washington Agricultural College and School of Science.

For starters, there's the portrait of him that hangs in the lobby of Bryan Hall. The eyes in this portrait unnervingly follow visitors as they walk around the lobby, and sometimes Bryan turns his head in their direction—or so it's said, anyway.

Bolstering the connection between Bryan and the otherworldly is the assertion that he was fond of telling ghost stories in his day. Furthermore, the college president died one week after Halloween in 1941, and reputedly his funeral was held in the building that was later named in his honor.

Whether or not they are connected directly to Bryan's ghost, a number of other inexplicable events have been reported in various parts of Bryan Hall over the years. Among the most notable of these are chimes that ring in the middle of the night, a chair that rocks by itself, strange moans and whistles, and doors that lock and unlock on their own.

And then there's the stage used for musical and dramatic performances, which seems to be an especially popular locale for Bryan's resident spirits. Among the inexplicable events that have been reported there are several occasions when big stage lights unaccountably fell from the rafters and crashed to the stage, narrowly missing anyone unlucky enough to be standing underneath them.

One of Bryan Hall's custodians, Aaron McArthur, says that he was frightened at first of such spirits but in general remains a skeptic. He told *WSU Today* reporter Cynthia King, "When I first got here, the theater kind of creeped me out. But every building has its weird noises. . . . If you psych yourself up, you can scare yourself with anything."

On the other hand, spooky encounters have made some-thing of a believer out of Richard Uthmann, an alumnus of the university's music department. Uthmann recalled in a piece for the school's *Our Story* website that he was Bryan's stage manager in the late 1950s. He stated that it was his habit to aim and focus the stage lights after the building closed for the night, in anticipation of the next day's performances.

Uthmann noted in his essay that the large stage lights he would put into position were located in the ceiling of the auditorium. The only way to get to them was by climbing up Bryan's bell tower to the third floor and then going through a heavy steel fire door. This route led to a loft over the audi-torium, which in addition to the heavy stage lights was also used to store stage props and other large items.

When Uthmann first started working at Bryan, he went up into the loft with one of the school's faculty members to get an orientation. While they were up there, Uthmann noticed an antique rocking chair sitting by itself out in the middle of the floor. He picked it up, thinking that he would stack it with the rest of the chairs near the walls. But the instructor told the new manager to leave the chair where it was. Once upon a time, he explained, it had been the chair most favored by Enoch A. Bryan and that out of respect he, the instructor, liked to keep it right where it was. Uthmann was skeptical, but he was a student—he couldn't ignore a faculty member. So he did as he was told and left the chair where it was.

The next time Uthmann had occasion to go up into the loft, he went alone. As would be expected, the chair was still out in the middle of the room by itself. This time, Uthmann took matters into his own hands and moved it over against the wall with the loft's other chairs.

The student then went on about his task, putting the lights into their correct positions. It was late at night and no one else was in the building. Uthmann was sure of this because the janitor went home as he, Uthmann, was still working in the loft. The janitor asked the new manager to lock the doors as he left.

Then came the strange bit. While he was still working on the lights, Uthmann heard a nearby heavy fire door open and close, but when he looked he saw no one there. He paid little attention to it, assuming that it was simply the janitor checking on him. Then, a moment later, Uthmann suddenly became extremely cold, to the point of shivers and chattering teeth—even though he was standing right next to a very hot carbon arc light. The sensation of intense cold passed as quickly as it had arrived, and Uthmann was able to finish the rest of the lights quickly and without anything unusual happening.

But then came a real surprise: When he went back through the fire door, the rocking chair that had been E. A. Bryan's favorite—the one he had just moved—was again sitting in the middle of the floor, empty but rocking away. Being no fool, Uthmann left it where it was. As he related in his essay, "I watched for a minute, but it didn't stop. The air around it was cold, but I wasn't brave enough to touch the chair. I'm not sure I believe in ghosts, but I never moved that chair unless it was necessary to move props, and then it went right back in the right spot. Many times later when I went up there, no matter if it was night or day, the chair was moving slightly, but I never felt the cold again.

"Some things you just don't mess with."

Meanwhile, down in the basement of Bryan Hall—or the catacombs, as it's often called—is another unfathomable mystery. A part of the dirt floor down there has a number of small mounds that could be construed as graves. Could they be the graves of students who have left the school under mysterious circumstances? Or possibly of Native Americans who once lived in the region? Chances are good that we'll never know.

While we're visiting the WSU campus, let's not forget some of the other buildings that are said to be haunted.

For one, there's the Owen Science and Engineering Library. This facility is in a relatively modern building (it opened in 1977), but it may nonetheless harbor a spooky presence or two. Specifically, many people have reported that the third floor of the library is much colder and creepier than the rest of the building. (Don't listen to those who will tell you that for some reason the third floor got less insulation than the rest of the building when under construction. Some people just like to spoil good stories.)

And then there's Daggy Hall, which also dates from the 1970s and houses, among other things, two performing arts theaters. Some people say that Daggy has its own resident ghosts.

As possible evidence, reporter King notes, the construction of Daggy Hall was somewhat haphazard, so that in the building there are several doors, stairs, and hallways that end abruptly or lead to nowhere—perfect haunting grounds for resident spirits.

Interviewed by King in 2005, Daggy Hall custodian Arron McMullen reported that he often heard odd creaking noises when the heating and ventilation systems turned on shortly after his daily arrivals in the early morning. Ben Gonzales, a theater instructor at the university, is skeptical about the idea that such noises might indicate anything strange. He points out that the various systems that maintain a building—mechanical, hydraulic, electronic, ventilation, and so on—frequently make strange noises, for perfectly rational reasons, and don't always behave as expected.

Despite this skeptical note, however, Gonzales adds that he has had some unsettling and bizarre experiences at Daggy. He's heard mysterious sounds of running feet, and both he and the stage manager distinctly heard children's voices backstage in one of the building's theaters at 3:30 a.m. Gonzales told King, "When you're in this building late at night, you definitely get a feeling you're not the only person here."

And then there's the ghost story connected to the original Ferry Hall, the first large building to be constructed on the WSU campus as a dorm. (This structure burned in 1897 and was replaced by another building that stood until the mid-1970s. The only remaining bit of the original buildings is the former bell tower, now a gazebo next to Murrow Hall.)

It's said that in the bleak, snowy, and windy dead of winter (it gets really cold in Pullman), a white, formless ghostly shape, floating in the air, was seen near Ferry Hall for several nights in a row. According to an undated story reprinted on the university website, "It did not reach to the ground by two or three feet. It seemed to rise and fall. Occasionally it disappeared entirely."

The spirit always came at the same hour of the evening: soon after 11:00 p.m., when lights went out in the dormitory. According to legend, the ghostly presence could only be glimpsed, since it disappeared whenever anyone tried to approach. One brave student armed with a loaded revolver tried to go very near; the student fired when he saw what looked like the apparition, but the ghost vanished without a trace and hasn't been seen since.

On the other hand, who's to say the spirit isn't still around, perhaps biding its time to avenge being shot at so rudely?

Finally, no visit to the WSU campus would be complete without a nod to Lara Cummings, one of the school's librarians. The outgoing Cummings leads ghost tours of the Holland and Terrell libraries for students and the public, during which she shrieks, howls, and jumps out from behind bookshelves to spice up the stories she relates.

But Cummings's tours aren't just meant to scare your socks off. They also allow her to teach people how to navigate through the stairwells, elevators, bookshelves, and hallways of two extensive, interconnected research facilities. She figures that there's no reason why library tours have to be dull. One student, quoted in a 2012 *WSU News* press release, concurs: "She's hilarious. Who'd have guessed it could be so fun to learn their way around a library?"

Among the stories the librarian tells on her hour-long tours is one about a ghost seen floating on the grounds of Old College Hall (now the site of Murrow Hall). According to legend, another otherworldly presence is the spirit of a library worker who died of cancer—but who continues to write answers to students' questions, putting them on cards dropped inside a box near her old office.

A ghostly librarian!

SPOKANE

North of WSU's home in Pullman is Eastern Washington's biggest city, Spokane. Many of the supernatural stories told in Spokane revolve around another institution of higher learning: Gonzaga University. But before we get into them, here's a curious little tidbit:

Bing Crosby, Spokane's most famous son, dropped out of Gonzaga, where he had planned to be a lawyer, to pursue a career in music. (In retrospect, it was a pretty good move.)

Over the years, Der Bingle memorably recorded a number of songs with titles that would seem to fit in with the subject at hand. Among these tunes: "I Don't Stand a Ghost of a Chance with You," "The Yodeling Ghost," and "Ghost Riders in the Sky."

Coincidence? You be the judge.

MONAGHAN HALL

Monaghan Hall is a beautiful old house that today serves as Gonzaga's music building. (In fact, it's often called simply the Music Mansion.) But music is apparently not the only thing wafting through its halls.

The building is named in honor of James Monaghan, an Irish immigrant and early resident of Spokane who completed its construction in 1901 to serve as his home. Monaghan made a respectable small fortune, beginning with hauling freight and trading with other early settlers and the indigenous Indian tribes before moving on to supplying the US Army with food and stores as they expanded its operations in the Pacific Northwest. By the time of his death in 1916, Monaghan was a well-respected businessman with holdings in real estate, railroads, and mining.

Today, the Monaghan Mansion is the centerpiece of an enduring legend that still evokes curiosity and chills. Generations of Gonzaga students, faculty, and visitors have paused in front of the mansion to meditate on the many reports made over the years of inexplicable events.

The legend of Monaghan Mansion includes the lore that James Monaghan was murdered in his home (not true), and the possibly true information that the ghostly music heard decades later in the building is the same as that played at Monaghan's funeral.

The many reports of ghostly happenings in the mansion include many elements of a "typical" haunted house: cold spots, mysterious footsteps and strange noises coming from unoccupied areas, blackboards moving by themselves, lights and doors spontaneously turning on or opening, music (specifically from an organ and a flute) wafting late at night from empty rooms, and an overall presence of something evil—or at least really creepy.

Many people have wondered if these events were caused by the spirit of the late owner. Or could they be the work of the ghostly presence of Monaghan's celebrated son?

That young man was John Robert Monaghan, who was in the first graduating class of Gonzaga University and the first Washingtonian to graduate from the Naval Academy in Annapolis, Maryland. John Robert died during the Spanish-American War aboard the USS *Philadelphia* in 1899, apparently while helping a fellow sailor when they were caught in a gun battle in Samoa. Ensign John Robert Monaghan is almost as honored a figure in Spokane as his father; a statue of him, erected in 1906, stands at the corner of Riverside and Monroe.

Could either—or both—Monaghans be the source of the strange events at their former home? Or could it be someone else? According to some reports, the Monaghan Mansion's spirit may be that of a young seminarian who reportedly hanged himself in the building's attic. (Some versions of this story identify the suicide as a Gonzaga student who was not studying for the priesthood.)

The stories about the presence of a ghost in the Music Mansion really began to pile up in the 1970s. Notable among these were the experiences related by a security guard. He reported that he worked with a partner identified only as "Paul." Both were former military men. Among their other jobs, at the end of each day they routinely turned off the lights, closed windows, and locked the mansion at midnight. . . . But the morning people discovered on several occasions that the building's doors were mysteriously found open and the lights still on.

In addition, the two security guards witnessed something strange as they were locking up the upstairs attic one night. A wheeled blackboard propelled itself up behind the narrator without a sound, travelling across a squeaky old wooden floor. The guard who reported this thought at first that Paul was playing a practical joke, but they were thirty feet apart—too far for Paul to have moved the blackboard without a sound.

According to a 2005 article in the *Gonzaga University Bulletin* by Liz Merrill, the reports of these and other eerie incidents grew so persistent that in 1974 a group of students urged Father Walter Leedale, then an associate professor of music at the school, to perform an exorcism of the building.

Father Leedale was skeptical at first. Nonetheless, he agreed to sleep in his office in the mansion overnight. What he reported was an unnerving night full of strange noises— he barely slept at all. In the morning, when he went to unlock one of the doors, the doorknob turned by itself and the door opened by what he felt was a hostile, invisible presence. Needless to say, there was no one there.

The overall experience was so frightening, in fact, that he was inspired to embark on further investigation. By the time he reached the end of this inquiry, the priest later said, he had changed his mind—he was convinced that the rumors were based in fact, and that the place was indeed haunted.

In addition to his alarming night in the mansion, several other mysterious events he personally experienced convinced Father Leedale that the place did indeed harbor a spirit. On one occasion, for instance, he heard a flautist playing a haunting melody. He searched the building but found it empty. Later, as he played a different melody on the piano, one of the building's housekeepers told him that she had returned to the empty house to retrieve a forgotten item one night and heard the same melody while alone in the building.

Intrigued, the housekeeper followed the sound to the organ room, which was securely locked. She opened the door and peeked in the room, and the organ's keys and mechanism were moving—by themselves. Around the same time, there were reports of unnerving sounds of growling emanating from an empty basement storage area.

On another occasion, both Father Leedale and a security guard heard a series of growling sounds coming from the other side of a locked door in the building. Upon examination, the room contained only a cello with broken strings and, bizarrely, an axe embedded in a block of wood—nothing that would cause a growling sound.

Still another strange incident was an occasion when Father Leedale, music department chair Daniel Brenner, and two security guards all felt a tingly presence as they were in the building together. One of the security guards said that he felt as though he was strangling. Both guards felt cold hands trying to strangle them, and Brenner was unable to move beyond the threshold. (Various versions of the story differ in the details of who experienced what symptoms.)

That was the convincer. After investigating this and other incidents, Father Leedale and Brenner became convinced that they had to intervene. In February 1974 or 1975 (sources differ), the priest and his colleague conducted a formal four-day ceremony to cleanse the house of spirits. The ceremony, called a blessing, in some ways closely resembles the rites of exorcism that the Catholic Church uses to cleanse people and places of evil demons.

According to Father Leedale, the blessing was quite an event. The priest stated that during the ceremony a crucifix around his neck swung back and forth on its own, sometimes so violently that he had to hold on to it with one hand as he grasped his prayer book with the other. In 1994, Leedale told the *Pacific Northwest Inlander* newspaper, "Honest to God, I don't know what it was, but I can say that Christians believe there are evil forces in the world, and that we, as Christians, pray to God to protect us from them, or for the strength to deal with them. This is what I was doing at the music building."

It appeared to the priest at the time as if his blessing ceremony had been successful, and that the spirit had left. But since then there have been more reports and rumors of strange doings. One campus worker told reporter Merrill, "Some campus employees I work with went into the mansion at night. Now at least two of these people refuse to enter the mansion; even to this day they won't go in it."

Furthermore, there have been reports that a local historian went to what was then the Cheney Cowles Museum in Spokane in search of photos of the mansion and the Monaghan family. (The Cheney Cowles is now the Northwest Museum of Arts and Culture, maintained by the Eastern Washington State Historical Society.)

According to this story, the researcher stopped her work when she made a chilling discovery. She uncovered a photo of John Robert Monaghan's casket as it lay in state in the family home. The casket was elaborately draped in black and decorated with crucifixes, as is standard practice among some Catholics—but the crucifixes were all upside down, the symbol of St. Peter. To some, the appearance of an upside-down cross is associated with Satanism.

Whether or not the photo of the casket has anything to do with anti-religious sentiments, the rumors about Monaghan Mansion persist to this day, despite the school authorities' attempts to dispel them and emphasize the positive aspects of Gonzaga's music program housed in a beautiful old mansion. Still, is there something spooky going on in Monaghan Hall?

THE DAVENPORT HOTEL

Outside of Gonzaga, perhaps the most famous Spokane haunting is the legend about that city's Davenport Hotel, built in 1914 and today restored to its original elegance. Over the years there have been many reports emanating from the Davenport of many different phenomena.

By far, the best known of the Davenport's spooky stories is the sad tale of Ellen McNamara. A wealthy widow from New York, Mrs. McNamara met an untimely demise at the hotel on August 17, 1920, under very strange circumstances. Ever since, a rumor has persisted that she never quite left the building.

Ellen—can we call her that?—was, at the time, on a lengthy tour of the American West with her sister and two cousins. On their travels, they stopped overnight in Spokane, en route to Montana's Glacier National Park, when fate stepped in.

According to the story, Ellen felt unwell around dinnertime that night and chose to take the air on the hotel's third floor balcony instead of joining the rest of her party as they dined on the main floor. The next thing anyone knew, a powerful crash was heard coming from the lobby. Ellen had fallen through a Tiffany glass skylight, high above the lobby court—and she landed hard.

The front-page headline in the *Spokane Spokesman-Review* of the next day excitedly announced, "Matron Falls to Death Through Hotel Skylight." The anonymous newspaper writer who reported on the crash noted, "Witnesses of the fall said the woman's shoulder struck the floor first and that her head crashed against the stone. Perhaps 100 persons saw her fall. Several men rushed to her and carried her to a couch. She was conscious for a few seconds and asked, 'Where did I go?' before she became insensible."

A doctor who had been in the hotel's dining room, John O'Shea, examined the unconscious woman before moving her to her room. She died about an hour later of massive head trauma. No one knows why she fell, although there is speculation that she somehow opened a door that led directly to the glass roof and, mistaking its checkerboard pattern for a floor, stepped out on it. (Why there was a door that led directly to a glass ceiling is unclear.) In any case, the incident was apparently an accident; there was no indication that Ellen might have been contemplating suicide.

Under normal circumstances, this tragic event would no doubt have remained forgotten in history. Instead, the belief that Mrs. McNamara's ghost still lingers in the hotel has become an enduring legend, one with many variations. Among those reporting sightings of the dead woman's ghost are a number of housekeepers who say they have glimpsed a lady in a black dress, as well as guests and other staff who say that the dead woman still walks the hotel's halls and mezzanine. Dressed either in white or black (depending on who's telling the story), the spirit has been known to stop people passing by and plaintively ask, "Where did I go?"

Perhaps not coincidentally, the legend of Ellen McNamara has been excellent business for the Davenport. *Spokesman-Review* writer Doug Clark wryly noted in 2005, "Having a guest crash through a skylight onto a crowded floor isn't the sort of check-out hotels normally want publicized. But management at Spokane's luxurious Davenport Hotel has determined the deadly descent of Ellen McNamara qualifies as a rare exception to the rule."

But Ellen's ghost is by no means the only spirit said to haunt the Davenport. There's also the spirit responsible for such phenomena as inexplicable cigar smoke and heavy, clearly male footsteps heard on the marble floor of the lobby, very early in the morning or very late at night when no one but the witness is present.

Who could it be? Well, for one thing, it's widely rumored that the ghost of the hotel's founder, Llewellyn (Louis) Davenport, regularly roams the halls of his beloved facility. A known perfectionist, Davenport regularly made his rounds of room inspections and checking the halls floor by floor, very early in the morning and very late at night . . . and perhaps still does, cigar in hand.

According to the legend, Davenport often stated while alive, "I never want to leave here." He got his wish: Both the hotel owner and his wife died in Suite 1105—or at least their earthly presence went away. Not surprisingly, it's said that their otherworldly presence can still be felt in that very spot.

Many guests have reported eerie experiences while staying in the suite, such as items that mysteriously move and appliances that turn on and off without being plugged in. On one occasion, a couple from Alaska was staying there over New Year's Eve and attended a downstairs party. When they went back to their room, they left their noisemakers on the counter, only to awake in the morning and find them on the floor. They put them back on the counter and went to breakfast—and when they returned, the noisemakers were back on the floor.

Okay, a little strange. But then they put them on the counter and went shopping downtown. When they returned, the maid had cleaned their room, and it was spotless . . . except that the noisemakers were on the floor once again.

Guests are not the only ones to have felt Louis Davenport's presence. The hotel's communications director, Tom McArthur, told writer Paul Seebeck for a 2005 article in the *Pacific Northwest Inlander,* "Construction workers and electricians were working on the 11th floor before the hotel opened [after a major renovation]. The windows were sealed and closed. There was no cross breeze. One of them said, 'Isn't this where the Davenports had their personal suite?' At that moment, the wiring started swinging to and fro."

But Louis Davenport and Ellen McNamara aren't the only spirits hanging around the old hotel. Persistent stories exist about a ghost seen near the Davenport's spa facility. Specifically, staff members have reported seeing a man in formal attire with what appears to be a white towel hanging over his arm. Under the impression that he may be a guest who is lost, the staffers have walked toward him—only to watch in puzzlement as he disappeared. Perhaps, McArthur speculates, it's the ghost of a formally dressed butler, towel at the ready, waiting for his employer to appear from the spa.

And there are plenty of other stories as well. Consider, for example, the reports of bellmen who greet guests and then disappear into the air. And at least one bellman, very much still living, says he has witnessed something eerie himself. Quoted by Seebeck, Michael Peterson recalled that just before Christmas one year he felt something strange while helping a guest to his room: "I was pulling a heavy bell cart. Suddenly, it was being pushed by someone. I felt the biggest chill up my back. I was just spooked."

Peterson went on to tell Seebeck that he remembered exactly where he was that night: "I was on the East Wing of the 10th floor, on my way to room 1015. I've gone back to that spot, trying to figure out what happened. I don't normally believe in ghosts, or anything, but I believe something was there."

Maintenance worker Harvey Hudson also remembered one unnerving night when he was on the fourth floor. Quoted by Seebeck, Hudson stated, "I heard a loud noise, and saw that a terrace door had flown wide open. I walked out. There was nobody there."

It wasn't a windy night, Hudson recalled, and the door, made of heavy metal and glass, had been latched. Hudson went on, "There's no way that door could've opened by itself. I'm a grown man, but I didn't go back there for a week. I can't explain it. It gave me goose bumps."

Seebeck also related the testimony of Kara Trail, who supervised the flower shop. She was getting the hotel ready for Christmas one evening, she asserted, when she walked into a completely empty ballroom late one night: "Suddenly, I felt really creepy and noticed there was dead silence. Then I heard a shuffling sound. I looked at the curtains, but they were fastened at top and bottom—not moving. Later a coworker told me, 'Oh, that was just people dancing.'"

And Seebeck also quoted Sharon Hunter, one of the hotel's concierges. Hunter commented, "I haven't had the visit for some time, but in my first year and half, every single shift I would feel like somebody was approaching." Hunter recalled experiencing a powerful sense that she should look up—but when she did there was nothing to see. "Always I would feel a presence around me, almost like a shadow," she stated, adding that it was her belief that what she sensed may have been Louis Davenport urging her to pay attention to approaching guests.

All in all, much of the Davenport's staff (and many of its guests as well) believe strongly in the hotel's reputation for being haunted by ghosts—ghosts that are, for the most part, playful and benign. McArthur, the communications director, told Seebeck, "As an official spokesperson of the hotel, I can never say, 'We have ghosts or don't have ghosts.' But based on what enough people have told me, we might."

McArthur went on to state that he believes Louis Davenport's "legacy of supreme hospitality" is what really haunts the building, helping to maintain the hotel's reputation for excellence. But McArthur also holds open the possibility that something supernatural is also at work: "The law of physics says energy is neither created nor destroyed. If you believe that, where does all this human energy go? Maybe it's still alive, in this same physical space that has all this human history."

MORE FROM SPOKANE

After checking out the Davenport Hotel (and perhaps checking out of it as well), ghost aficionados will be interested in visiting some of Spokane's other spooky locales. One of these is the River Park Square Mall—specifically, people report hearing whispering sounds near the bank of escalators leading to the AMC movie theater complex. Writing in the *Gonzaga University Bulletin* in 2010, Emily Nadal commented, "It's easy to get vertigo going up the steep escalators to AMC, and now it seems like whispering voices might be a new fear." These voices, it's said, exist because in 2003 a man committed suicide by jumping off the top escalator.

Similar eerie sounds and shadows have reportedly occurred on the fifteenth floor of Spokane's Double Tree Hotel. Some say the spirit of a guest who committed suicide is the cause of the disturbances. Other versions of the story attribute the sounds and shadows to a long-ago party that got out of hand.

Still another of Spokane's ghostly legends revolves around its venerable Greenwood Cemetery. Of particular interest is the steep, century-old flight of stairs, the "Thousand Steps," leading to the cemetery. These steps can be found at the cemetery's side entrance. The story goes that anyone who tries to climb the stairs will be accosted by— you guessed it—a variety of otherworldly spirits.

According to legend, these ghosts are so terrifying that no one has ever been able to get completely to the top. At least, no one still living has made the climb. . . .

And then there's the Patsy Clark mansion. Built in 1897 for a wealthy mining mogul (Patsy was a man, by the way), the beautifully restored, fourteen-thousand-square-foot mansion was for some time a restaurant and now is a reception hall and the offices of a law firm. According to the stories told about it, ghostly music can be heard inside the mansion, apparently left over from the lavish parties that Clark and his family loved to hold. As for specific spirits, Patsy's wife Mary is apparently still in residence. She's been sighted by many people over the years, wearing period attire and floating around the house.

Dating from the days when the mansion was a restaurant, there's a tale that a busboy had been clearing tables upstairs one day when something very strange occurred. According to a 2011 article by KXLY4 reporter Annie Bishop, the busboy was walking down the main staircase and was nearly to the main floor when he felt a clammy presence behind him. He paused, looked behind, and saw a figure floating down the staircase. As it drew near, the apparition vanished.

Meanwhile, the mansion's dank basement was formerly the restaurant's extensive wine cellar. That chamber is today reportedly the most haunted room in the mansion. It's said that wine bottles and glasses have mysteriously shattered and moved back and forth in the air on their own.

All of these many stories make it clear that Spokane has for many years been one of the most haunted cities in Washington. Why? Only the Shadow knows.

CHENEY

Less than twenty miles southwest of Spokane is Cheney, best known to the world as the home of Eastern Washington University. And the home of at least one ghost.

First up is the story of the spirit that plagued Elizabeth McLanahan way back at the turn of the twentieth century—and that has gone on to plague modern-day toilets.

Mrs. McLanahan was a widow who lived in a house at 321 Sixth, diagonally across the street from EWU (or the Cheney State Normal School, as it was known then). In 1909, it seems, she was plagued for months by a pesky spirit—so much so that she offered a reward for its capture. She offered fifteen dollars—a tidy sum for the times, especially for a widow who made her living doing laundry. She circulated a notice around town (reprinted in a 2009 *Spokane Spokesman-Review* article by Jonathan Brunt) that read: "Fifteen dollars reward will be paid to any one that will locate and identify a party prowling around my back door and yard and kitchen windows evenings from near 7 till 9 o'clock. A view may be had from both streets and alley. This is not a freak of imagination. The sneak does exist, but is ghostlike, as he seems to float far out and near and does not seem to wear any shoes."

The story made the news. The *Spokesman-Review* of October 31, 1909, included an article with this headline: "Ghost seen at Cheney. Woman fears strange specter that haunts cottage."

(Do you think it was a coincidence that the story appeared in the paper on Halloween?)

There's no mention in later records that anyone claimed this reward. Whether or not she solved her problem, Mrs. McLanahan sold the house in 1917 (the house no longer exists) and moved elsewhere. One of the homes she occupied in later years burned to the ground in the 1970s. Reporter Brunt wondered in his piece, "Did McLanahan move to get away from the spirit? Was the ghost responsible for burning down her former home on Fourth decades later? What about the fire that destroyed the main building at the Normal School in 1912?"

Brunt visited the site where McClanahan's haunted house once stood and spoke with Britney Dancer, who works across the street in EWU's visitor center. Asked if she had ever experienced any paranormal activity there, she said yes. Sometimes, she said, the toilets in the visitor center will flush on their own.

Meanwhile, residents of the small building that stands where McLanahan's house once was have little to report. Quoted in Brunt's story, one student who lived there stated, "I'm sure I've heard some bumps in the night, but you never know if it's your neighbors."

Be that as it may, there have been no reports of ghosts near the old McLanahan home in recent decades. Brunt concludes, "If the ghost that haunted Elizabeth McLanahan at her Cheney home in 1909 is still around, he's not doing much harm. Unless you're concerned about needlessly depleting the water supply."

On the EWU campus itself, meanwhile, there have been reports of many ghostly presences. Dancer told Brunt about a screaming woman's face that has been spotted in a dormitory window. There are also enduring legends that the school's Monroe Hall and Senior Hall are haunted by spirits who are known to screech, bang doors, and otherwise make their presence known.

Over at Streeter Hall, a co-ed residence hall on campus, it's said that the ghost of a workman who fell to his death in 1967, during the construction of the hall, still lingers. Students affectionately nicknamed the spirit Lucky. For better or worse, the story isn't true. One workman, Theron McAda, did fall several stories during construction, but he survived. Still, the legend is passed on from one generation of students to the next that his spirit still wanders the corridors of Streeter Hall.

WALLA WALLA

The creaky old joke about Walla Walla is that it's the city so nice they named it twice. Actually, the name comes from the Native American tribe who once lived there, one of the many Indian groups Lewis and Clark encountered on their famous journey. The name is usually translated as "Many Waters."

Well, Walla Walla, on the banks of the mighty Columbia River in the far southeast of the state, really is a nice city, best known to the world as the home of Whitman College, a number of award-winning wineries, and Walla Walla sweet onions. (Also, ominously enough, it's the site of the Washington State Penitentiary, the site of the state's death row and thus the locale, as of 2012, for seventy-eight executions since the early twentieth century.)

Walla Walla was settled by white pioneers in the 1830s and incorporated in the 1860s, so not surprisingly it boasts some handsome Victorian-era buildings. Also not surprising is that some of them are said to be haunted.

One of the more interesting buildings in town is the Kirkman House on the corner of Colville and Cherry. It was built by a prominent pioneer couple, William and Isabelle Kirkman (some sources name her as Isabella). The Kirkmans finished building the place in 1880 and raised four children there. (Another five kids, tragically, did not survive into adulthood.) William, a textile merchant and a native of England, died in 1893, and his funeral services were held in the home. According to reports of the time, there were so many mourners during the ceremony and subsequent viewing that the crowd spilled out to the grounds around the house and the surrounding streets. After his death, William's widow continued to live in the house for years. She donated it to Whitman College in 1919 and passed away in her native Ireland in 1931.

As with so many vintage buildings, the imposing brick mansion was for a time used for a variety of mundane purposes but fell into neglect for years. In the 1970s, it was acquired by a group of Walla Walla citizens interested in preserving and restoring it to its original elegant condition, and the Kirkman House today is a museum with permanent displays recreating life in Victorian times.

Among the museum's displays are several pictures of Isabelle. In these she was stiffly posed, as was usual for photo sessions of the day, but nonetheless she gives the impression of having been a calm and gentle person. In other words, she doesn't seem at first glance to be a scary presence—so who would think of her as having the potential to haunt the place?

And yet stories persist that Isabelle's spirit remains there, the cause of numerous strange doings.

Sure, one of the mysterious sounds turned out to be nothing spookier than a paper shredder, according to a 2011 blog entry by Susan Monahan for Tourism Walla Walla's website. Monahan also mentions reports of other seemingly unexplainable events that proved to have mundane and boring explanations. One such was a motion detector sensor that went off on its own, making a loud noise. It turned out that the cause was nothing more than the wind leaking in.

On the other hand, some of the home's other reported mysteries are just that—mysteries.

One of these inexplicable events occurred during one of the museum's popular fundraising events, the annual

Whispered Memories Psychic Teas. (Psychic dinners have also been held there.) Hosted by Janice Lynch, a psychic from nearby Kennewick, these teas aim to connect guests with their departed loved ones. Such séances were often held in Victorian times, although there's no indication that the Kirkman family ever conducted one. Kirsten Schober, the museum's executive director, told the *Walla Walla Union-Bulletin* in 2009, "People during the Victorian Era were just fascinated with the idea of the supernatural and were seeking scientific exploration of the metaphysical occurrences."

Of course, psychic events are by their very nature unexplainable. But Monahan described one in particular, when the dining room lights flickered when a participant asked a question of someone on the Other Side.

Otherwise, the strange occurrences at the mansion include mysterious noises, footsteps scurrying down the main hallway, mysteriously locked or unlocked doors, disembodied voices that speak to guests in the lobby, a mist at the bottom of the stairs, disappearing or hidden keys, lights turned off at the end of the day (especially those in Isabelle's bedroom) and TV remotes (used for audio-visual displays) that flip themselves across rooms.

Monahan's favorite story, she wrote, concerned a friend of hers who sits on the museum's board of directors. This woman was working alone in the upstairs office at 3:00 p.m. when she heard an odd noise and followed the sound into a bedroom. Monahan noted, "She described it as not having a recognizable face but as 'human' in form and clothed in swirling drapery. And it giggled. And giggled. And followed my friend when she left the room."

Monahan's friend welcomed it to Kirkman House, apparently not considering that it might have been there long before she showed up. The woman followed it around a bit, and then told the spirit goodbye, explaining that she had work to do: "The spirit followed her into the office, swirled around the room a few times, and then disappeared. And my friend got back to work."

DAYTON

Just up the road from Walla Walla to the northeast is the town of Dayton, which is the seat of Columbia County. One of Dayton's restored buildings from earlier years is today the elegant Weinhard Hotel. Dating from 1890, it's named for a local brewer, a German named Jacob Weinhard, who was a pretty big deal in Dayton back in the day. He established a brewery, a malt house, a saloon and lodge hall, and a theater. Clearly a canny businessman, he also owned an interest in the local bank.

These days, the hotel has been the site of numerous reports of unusual paranormal activity. For example, guests staying in Room 16 have reportedly seen and spoken with the spirit of a young girl. Meanwhile, according to another story, an employee once spotted a blurry, distorted figure on the stairs.

Furthermore, in Room 11, a guest who forgot her key returned to find that two deadbolts had locked behind her—including one that she didn't have a key for. And a guest staying in Room 12 allegedly noticed a depression on the side of her bed she hadn't slept on. At first she figured it had been left by her dog, which was in the room with her, and she thought nothing of it. But then she noticed that the dog was on the floor, staring at the depression. As the guest watched, the depression disappeared and the dog, growling, tracked with its eyes something invisible that was apparently moving across the room.

Just another chilling day of ghosts at the Weinhard Hotel!

Epilogue

The tales in this book are just a sample of the true scope of ghost stories that have haunted Washington for many decades. Countless other reports of otherworldly appearances pepper the state—and make it an even more fascinating and attractive place to visit or make your home.

East, west, north, or south—from the rugged San Juan Islands of the upper left-hand corner to the dry plains of the state's southeast region, or from the mouth of the mighty Columbia River on the southwest coast to the remote far northeast. In the present day or in the distant past—from long-ago legends to up-to-the-minute shenanigans. No matter where you go in the state, or what period of time you take a look at, you're sure to encounter something bizarre— something that will send shivers up your spine, make your hair stand on end, cause your blood to run cold, just give you the creeps . . . or maybe every single one of those things.

Here's hoping that this book will inspire you to take your own journey of dreadful discovery around the region. You can start by searching out the details of the blood-curdling spectacles and chilling tales mentioned here. Then you can graduate to making your own exciting, eerie discoveries.

In any case, happy ghost trails!

Selected Bibliography

ARTICLES

Bagby, Cali. "High Heels, a Hanging and the Cry Baby House." *IslandsSounder,* October 31, 2012.

Bailey, Mike. "History Takes on Ghostly Air." The (Vancouver, WA) *Columbian,* October 19, 2007.

Baurick, Tristan. "Olalla's 'Starvation Heights' Still Causes Chills after a Century." *Kitsap Sun,* July 9, 2011.

Bock, Paula. "East Kong Yick Building." *Seattle Times,* August 12, 2005.

Caldbick, John. "Yacolt." Historylink.org, March 14, 2010.

Clark, Doug. "Davenport Ghost Has Roots in Fact." *Spokane Spokesman-Review,* August 17, 2005.

"Cleansing Ritual in Vancouver Puts Roaming Spirits to Rest." *Seattle Times,* June 27, 1993.

Crowley, Walt. "Burnley Ghost and Other Seattle Apparitions." Historylink.org, no date.

____. "Haunted Email from Rose Red." Historylink.org, no date.

Dizon, Kristin. "Ageless Beauty: The Allure of Lake Crescent Never Grows Old." *Seattle Post-Intelligencer,* August 9, 2001.

Eskenazi, Stuart. "Ghost Stories Haunt Pike Place Market." *Seattle Times,* June 13, 2008.

"Ghost Bar." *Seattle Weekly,* February 16, 2011.

Jackson, Jennifer. "Underground Tour Reveals Fort Worden's Dark Side." *Peninsula Daily News,* March 10, 2009.

Jasmin, Ernest A. "'Rimbauer' Writer Clears Up Book, Film Mystery." *Tacoma News Tribune,* February 2, 2003.

Jennings, Erin. "Port Gamble Ghost Conference to Discuss Things That Go Bump in the Night." *North Kitsap Herald,* October 21, 2011.

Gargas, Jane. "Holy Ghost—Does Spirit of Sister Sabina Inhabit St. Paul?" *Yakima Herald-Republic,* November 5, 2009.

Goffredo, Theresa. "Will 'Blithe Spirit' Conjure More Than One Ghost?" *Everett Herald,* September 23, 2011.

Green, Sara Jean. "Portraits of a Princess: Iconic Images of Chief Seattle's Eldest Daughter on Display." *Seattle Times,* July 13, 2001.

Grygriel, Chris. "Suicide—or Murder? 75th Anniversary of Pol's Sensational Death." *Seattle Post-Intelligencer,* August 30, 2011.

"Haunted Isle: Spooky Tales of Mercer Island's Past." *Mercer Island Reporter,* October 29, 2008.

Kehoe, Sarah. "Moses Lake Resident Believes Her Child Took Pictures of Ghosts." *Yakima Herald,* March 19, 2010.

"The Legend of the Black Cat." Washington State University *Our Story,* no date.

"Living History: Fort Ward Home Is Alive with WWII Secrets." *Bainbridge Island Review,* November 24, 2008.

Mapes, Diana. "Rats, Bats, Spiders and Spooks: Where the Wild Things Really Are." *Seattle Times,* October 27, 2005.

McNerthney, Casey. "Seattle History: The Shocking Murder at Green Lake." *Seattle Post-Intelligencer,* June 16, 2011.

Murakami, Kery. "Wah Mee: After 25 Years, Pain Lingers." *Seattle Post-Intelligencer,* February 18, 2008.

Oppegaard, Brett. "Simply Supernatural." (Clark County) *Columbian,* January 12, 1995.

Pascoe, Andrea. "A Halloween Tale: Mother, Daughter Discover 'Haunted' Home." *Ellensburg Daily Record,* October 31, 2003.

Peltin, Nena. "Home, Sweet Haunt." *SeattleMet,* July 22, 2012.

"Psychic to Seek the 'Souls' of Objects." *Walla Walla Union-Bulletin,* October 29, 2009.

"A Rich History." mountbakertheatre.com, no date.

Rosenow, Ty. "Myths Unveiled: The Social History of The Evergreen State College." http://evergreen.tyrosenow .com/MythsUnveiled.pdf.

Schwartz, Eric, and Dan Schreiber. "Creepy Haunts." *Lewis County Chronicle,* November 30, 2008.

Seebeck, Paul. "Haunted Hotel." *Pacific Northwest Inlander,* January 5, 2005.

Stein, Alan J. "Mercer Island's Calkins Hotel Burns to the Ground on July 2, 1908." Historylink.org, no date.

Watson, Kendall. "Halloween's Past Haunts Issaquah Business." *Issaquah Reporter,* December 19, 2011.

"Zombies Return to the Quiet Shores of Port Gamble." *North Kitsap Herald,* September 29, 2009.

SUGGESTED READING

Allison, Ross. *Spooked in Seattle.* Cincinnati: Clerisey, 2011.

"Athena," *Ghosts of Seattle.* Atglen, PA: Schiffer, 2008.

Davis, Jefferson. *Ghosts, Critters & Sacred Places of Washington and Oregon II.* Vancouver, WA: Norseman, 2005.

Dwyer, Jeff. *Ghost Hunter's Guide to Seattle and Puget Sound.* Gretna, LA: Pelican, 2008.

MacDonald, Margaret Read. *Ghost Stories from the Pacific Northwest.* Atlanta: August House, 2005.

Moffitt, Linda. *Washington's Haunted Hotspots.* Atglen, PA: Schiffer, 2009.

Smith, Barbara. *Ghost Stories of Washington.* Renton, WA: Lone Pine, 2000.

About the Author

Adam Woog, a Seattle native, has written many books for children, young adults, and adults. Among his books of Pacific Northwest history are *The Ballard Locks*; *Crossroads: The Experience Music Project Collection*; *Sexless Oysters and Self-Tipping Hats: 100 Years of Invention in the Pacific Northwest*; and *Atomic Marbles and Branding Irons: A Guide to Museums, Collections, and Roadside Attractions in Washington and Oregon* (with Harriet Baskas).

Woog also writes a monthly column on crime and mystery fiction for the *Seattle Times*, and he teaches at a preschool.

Woog lives in Seattle with his wife, Karen Kent. Their daughter, Leah, recently graduated from Arizona State University.